EVIDENCE-
TEACHING IN
PRIMARY EDUCATION

Critical Guides for
Teacher Educators

You might also like the following books from Critical Publishing.

Ability Grouping in Primary Schools: Case Studies and Critical Debates
Rachel Marks
978-1-910391-24-2

Beginning Teachers' Learning: Making Experience Count
Katharine Burn, Hazel Hagger and Trevor Mutton
978-1-910391-17-4

Coteaching in Teacher Education: Innovative Pedagogy for Excellence
Colette Murphy
978-1-910391-82-2

Developing Creative and Critical Educational Practitioners
Victoria Door
978-1-909682-37-5

Developing Outstanding Practice in School-Based Teacher Education
Edited by Kim Jones and Elizabeth White
978-1-909682-41-2

How Do Expert Primary Classteachers Really Work? A Critical Guide for Teachers, Headteachers and Teacher Educators
Tony Eaude
978-1-909330-01-6

Teacher Status and Professional Learning: The Place Model
Linda Clarke
978-1-910391-46-4

Theories of Professional Learning
Carey Philpott
978-1-909682-33-7

Our titles are also available in a range of electronic formats. To order please go to our website www.criticalpublishing.com or contact our distributor NBN International by telephoning 01752 202301 or emailing orders@nbninternational.com.

EVIDENCE-BASED
TEACHING IN
PRIMARY EDUCATION

Series Editor: Ian Menter

Critical Guides for
Teacher Educators

Edited by
Val Poultney

First published in 2017 by Critical Publishing Ltd

All rights reserved. No part of this publication may be reproduced, stored in a retrieval system, or transmitted in any form or by any means, electronic, mechanical, photocopying, recording or otherwise, without prior permission in writing from the publisher.

The authors have made every effort to ensure the accuracy of information contained in this publication, but assume no responsibility for any errors, inaccuracies, inconsistencies and omissions. Likewise every effort has been made to contact copyright holders. If any copyright material has been reproduced unwittingly and without permission the Publisher will gladly receive information enabling them to rectify any error or omission in subsequent editions.

Copyright © (2017) Jon Fordham, Helen Poultney, Val Poultney, Alison Richardson, Jacqui Trowsdale and Jennie White

British Library Cataloguing-in-Publication Data
A CIP record for this book is available from the British Library

ISBN: 9781911106463

This book is also available in the following ebook formats:

MOBI: 9781911106470
EPUB: 9781911106487
Adobe e-book reader: 9781911106494

The rights of Jon Fordham, Helen Poultney, Val Poultney, Alison Richardson, Jacqui Trowsdale and Jennie White to be identified as the Authors of this work have been asserted by them in accordance with the Copyright, Design and Patents Act 1988.

Cover and text design by Greensplash Limited
Project Management by Out of House Publishing
Typeset by Out of House Publishing
Print managed and manufactured by Jellyfish Solutions

Critical Publishing
3 Connaught Road
St Albans
AL3 5RX

www.criticalpublishing.com

Paper from responsible sources

To the memory of the late Andy Freeman who was an associate headteacher for Transform Trust, Nottingham. You were an inspirational teacher and a supporter of evidence-based teaching. You had a passion for research and finding new and exciting ideas to trial in the classroom. We, the staff of Allenton Community Primary School, dedicate this book to you.

CONTENTS

ACKNOWLEDGEMENTS

To everyone at Allenton Community Primary School, thank you for having the patience to work with me.

To Jon, for sharing our faith in this approach to school improvement and for valuable insights as we engaged with EBT. It has been a long but ultimately a fruitful journey.

To the children of Allenton Community Primary School, thank you for being so enthusiastic about taking part in the new approaches to learning that teachers have written about in this book.

To Dr Brian Hall for his grammatical guidance, wise counsel and indefatigable patience in proofreading the text.

And finally to Ian Menter, series editor, and Julia Morris of Critical Publishing for all their support in the preparation of this book.

Val Poultney, 2017

FOREWORD

Since launching the series *Critical Guides for Teacher Education* in 2014, the need for such volumes seems to have increased greatly. When we started the series, we were acutely aware that there were many parts of the world where teacher education was becoming increasingly diverse in its organisation, structure and curriculum. Furthermore, an increasing range of participants were being asked to take responsibility for supporting the introduction of new members into the profession and for ensuring their continuing learning and development. It is certainly my belief that earlier volumes in the series have helped enormously in providing the kinds of research-based insights that will support the development of high-quality teacher learning and development in whatever context it is taking place.

Over recent years there has also been a groundswell of interest in the idea of evidence-based teaching – or EBT as it is often referred to. In schools all around England, and indeed the rest of the UK and beyond, we have seen teachers seeking to improve their own teaching and the quality of education in their schools through gathering and analysing evidence. To some extent this has always been an element of good teaching practice, but, under the influence of these developments, such approaches have become both more systematic and more public, that is, they have involved professional sharing and learning.

Indeed, in similar vein, the widely cited report of the inquiry undertaken by the British Educational Research Association in collaboration with the Royal Society for the Arts, Manufacture and Commerce (BERA-RSA, 2014) has offered evidence for the importance of a systematic approach to the use of research and evidence in high-quality teacher education, including the learning of practising teachers. That report suggested that all teachers should have an entitlement to become 'research literate'.

It is therefore a great pleasure to introduce this volume to the series. It has been drawn together by Val Poultney, a university-based tutor, but is not her work alone. She has been working as an external facilitator with colleagues in Allenton Community Primary School, where the headteacher Jon Fordham and his colleagues have worked together to bring an EBT approach to their work. What is demonstrated in this book is how powerful such an approach may be not only in improving the quality of education in the school but also in supporting the professional learning and understanding of the teachers involved. This model of working in partnership to introduce inquiry and systematic investigation into working practices has also worked elsewhere (eg, Beckett, 2016) and may be seen to demonstrate the enactment of what Lawrence Stenhouse described many years ago as the model of the 'teacher as researcher' (Stenhouse, 1975).

It is my expectation and belief that this volume by Val Poultney and the school team will provide a highly accessible and inspiring example to colleagues in many other schools and universities in the development of school-based research literacy.

Ian Menter, series editor

Emeritus Professor of Teacher Education, University of Oxford

REFERENCES

Beckett, L (2016) *Teachers and Academic Partners in Urban Schools: Threats to Professional Practice.* London: Routledge.

BERA-RSA (2014) *Research and the Teaching Profession – Building Capacity for a Self-Improving Education System.* London: BERA. [online] Available at: bera.ac.uk.

Stenhouse, L (1975) *An Introduction to Curriculum Research and Development.* London: Heinemann.

About the series editor

Ian Menter is Emeritus Professor of Teacher Education and was formerly the Director of Professional Programmes in the Department of Education at the University of Oxford. He previously worked at the Universities of Glasgow, the West of Scotland, London Metropolitan, the West of England; and Gloucestershire. Before that, he was a primary school teacher in Bristol, England. His most recent publications include *A Literature Review on Teacher Education for the 21st Century* (Scottish Government) and *A Guide to Practitioner Research in Education* (SAGE). His work has also been published in many academic journals.

About the book editor

Val Poultney is a senior lecturer at the University of Derby. She teaches on initial teacher education and postgraduate programmes. Her research interests include school leadership and school governance with a particular focus on how to develop leadership to support teachers as researchers.

ABOUT THE **CONTRIBUTORS**

Jon Fordham became headteacher of Allenton Community Primary School in Derby when the school was placed in special measures. Jon has established the use of evidence-based teaching (EBT) to raise standards and promote learning throughout the school. His philosophy of children's character development, alongside the acquisition of knowledge, has resulted in raised aspirations within the community he serves. Jon encourages all staff to embrace and disseminate research projects regularly. This in turn has engaged learners and teachers alike, resulting in the school's well-embedded ethos of lifelong learning.

Helen Poultney is an assistant headteacher at Allenton Community Primary School and has been teaching for eight years. Her role focuses on teaching and learning predominantly in Key Stage 2. She is an experienced Year 6 teacher, and she is the school's advocate for EBT. She coordinates and supports staff research projects and has responsibility for organising dissemination events.

Alison Richardson is the ICT manager at Allenton Community Primary School, a middle leader and a Year 3 teacher. She has been teaching for four years across both Key Stages 1 and 2. She has developed a keen interest in EBT, and her specialism is literacy and music. She has worked with Jacqui Trowsdale on colour-coded writing as an initiative and as part of her contribution to EBT, and together they have widely disseminated this project across a number of different professional contexts.

Jacqui Trowsdale is a middle leader at Allenton Community Primary School, a coordinator of mathematics and an experienced Year 3 teacher. She has been teaching in primary schools for 11 years. She is responsible for analysing mathematics data across the whole school, looking for trends and opportunities to support teachers where necessary. Jacqui has been particularly interested in colour-coded writing as a piece of research, and she has been able to incorporate music in her practice to enhance learning of her children.

Jennie White is an assistant headteacher at Allenton Community Primary School, with responsibility for behaviour and using data to identify school trends. She is an experienced Year 6 teacher and manages assessment. Her role as EBT 'horizon scanner' gives her opportunity to source current research and practice that may have impact across the school, and she works closely with Helen Poultney to implement research projects with staff.

CHAPTER 1 | THE SELF-IMPROVING SCHOOL AND EVIDENCE-BASED TEACHING: THE VALUE OF RESEARCHING PRACTITIONERS

Val Poultney

CRITICAL **ISSUES**

- *Understanding the value of evidence-based approaches to teaching and learning;*
- *Opportunities for everyone engaging with evidence-based teaching approaches;*
- *Building research capacity and creating a third space;*
- *Challenges for researching primary schools.*

Introduction

Back in 2015, I (Val, HEI academic) spent an uncomfortable afternoon with a group of primary teachers and their headteacher (Jon) trying to convince them of the worth of evidence-based teaching (EBT). They were clearly feeling uncomfortable too because I failed to find common ground with them for at least the first hour. I had hoped a quick introduction with the likes of Lawrence Stenhouse and David Hargreaves would have done the trick (after all they must have known about these two academics and their writing from their own university days), but alas, it was all to no avail and the silence in the room was deafening. Eventually I was saved from further embarrassment when one teacher tentatively asked me what it was I was trying to explain; what exactly was it I was asking her to do differently? What changes could I offer her to her already 'good' practice as she saw it? It struck me at that point how far removed the group was from their own initial teacher training; after all they had in all probability been challenged to undertake research for their final dissertations while at university, yet here they were, patently not seeing the link between research and school improvement. I learnt a few lessons from that afternoon: mainly that teachers have a distrust of university academics and especially one that was not a primary specialist (I was a secondary teacher before becoming an academic). So how did I recover from this initial bruising experience? Well, I have a motto of 'keeping the faith' (I just keep going). Fortunately for me, Jon was keen to understand how some of his newly introduced initiatives were working, and it was clear that he could already see some value in EBT. Based on that flimsy agreement, we began to make plans for the next stage in what was to become a two-year journey, culminating in this book. We have all written about our experiences; how a group of practising teachers and their headteacher from a Derby City Community Primary School (supported by an academic from the local university) re-engaged with their own professional practice and gave EBT 'a go'.

Context for EBT

The value of teachers undertaking research into their own practice (also referred to as teacher inquiry or EBT) has been well documented over the course of many years, and much of this work has demonstrated how effective the outcomes of EBT can be on improving teaching and learning. This chapter provides an academic perspective to explain why primary schools should be more research-engaged in their work – not only with the 'raising standards' agenda in mind but also in providing the opportunity for teachers to engage with (and take responsibility for) their own professional development. It provides a fresh perspective on how staff in primary schools can begin to build their knowledge capacity that is specific to their own context and considers how building research knowledge can provide a foundation for change that is real, lasting and sustainable. It considers some of the key drivers needed for implementing an EBT culture and how the whole process can be sustained over a period of time. This type of work is not without its challenges, but there are many opportunities for real growth and development for teachers and teacher-leaders as well as the children themselves. Finally, the chapter outlines some of the opportunities for practitioners to disseminate their work within the wider local, regional, national and international context.

School-based research

There is much recent evidence to support the notion that self-improving schools should be researched-engaged and research-active (Goldacre, 2013; Greany, 2015; Stoll, 2015), but the real question is how can that be achieved. Many primary schools lack the architecture to support teachers who wish to research into their own practice, both from an organisational and a leadership perspective. There is, in such schools, a lack of capacity to support this type of work and – taking into account that there is no agreed knowledge base for teachers (Hargreaves, 1996) – a near 'perfect storm' for research *in*action. This is a troubling situation given that newly qualified teachers are urged to engage with research as part of their training. The Carter Review of Initial Teacher Training (2015) has made recommendations that EBT should form a substantial component of Initial Teacher Training (ITT) programmes and suggested that the teacher standards should be more explicit with regard to the importance of this type of work in teaching. However, the gathering of empirical data in classroom contexts is clearly not the way forward preferred by many teachers who often regard 'tips for teaching' and 'quick fixes' preferable to the systematic collection and analysis of research evidence. At a systems level, changes to the inspection regime give rise to uncertainties about how exactly to evidence school improvement beyond statistical data. There is no agreed body of knowledge akin to those in law or medicine that teachers may draw upon in their defence; Sheard and Sharples (2016) refer to this as the so-called *'knowledge-doing gap'*.

Proponents of the EBT approach argue that there should be equal collaboration between educational practitioners, policymakers and researchers and a link established between research outcomes that are seen to be effective in education and how such outcomes could be used in the real-world context of school practice. What might constitute effective school improvement is, arguably, fashionable, context-specific and based on small-scale samples which possibly have little impact on raising standards nationally. In today's context of fast-paced schooling, heads and teachers need to be able to plan and respond rapidly to change agendas imposed externally, without the time or space to fully evaluate the worth of the proposed change as it might impact on their school. EBT as a means of generating an evidential claim to knowledge is a powerful approach but possibly only as 'local knowledge' that is very much bound to school context and arguably harder to generalise except to those schools in comparable circumstances. What constitutes 'good' research evidence in these contexts is not for university academics to judge, but it should be recognised that these data are but a small part of a bigger picture on the school improvement landscape. If we are to be truly concerned with raising standards in primary schools, then there has to be something more in it for teachers beyond 'tips for teaching' and yet another new initiative. We would hope all teachers see themselves as professionals with a contribution to make to the continuing development of their learners and to the profession itself. Engaging with EBT is a way of providing focussed staff development that is meaningful to teachers and that helps to build a knowledge base to supplement the normal statistical school data. EBT helps to give teaching a real purpose – to instil a confidence in (and 're-professionalise') teachers; and it may reduce teacher attrition rates at the same time. It opens up opportunities for networking, dissemination and debates about the outcomes of teacher research and challenges teachers to adopt a more inquiring and reflective perspective on their work.

Generating capacity where everyone is a learner

Building and sustaining capacity for everyone to be a learner is one of the crucial roles of any primary school leadership team. These leadership teams become leaders of learning for all staff and children (Harris, 2014; Moss, 2008) where they develop the potential to change hearts and minds and encourage teachers to focus on their pedagogy in order to make learning happen. School leaders drive the development of a critical epistemological base for practice that provides scope for teachers to reflect upon and explore their own professional practice. Capacity building goes beyond organisation and structure, however; it allows practitioners to work together in new ways. It is about establishing trust between colleagues and a collective will to want to work together. School leaders are therefore charged with investing in changing the school climate so that they – teachers, support staff and children – become central to the work of teaching and learning with internal alignment of teams, structures and resourcing that supports the development of personal and interpersonal capacity. It is about creating a collective capacity where learning is an integral part of everyone's role in school: leaders, teachers, support staff, estate workers, parents and governors (Harris and Muijs, 2005). It is about creating an environment where teachers develop an analytical approach to their own practice and where they begin to see their classrooms through an analytical lens.

Recognising and understanding why a school might be in deficit capacity learning mode (such as a school in challenging circumstances) is also part of the school leadership role. A good school is one where children learn effectively, teachers teach effectively and where there is opportunity for everyone to learn. Sustaining this capacity for learning is an important role for the headteacher and leadership teams; they become leaders of learning (Harris, 2014; Moss, 2008). In the spirit of taking responsibility for improvement of learning, school leaders may avail themselves of an opportunity to work with an intermediary such as an HEI academic. This affords closer contact with current educational research that can be used to inform and drive inquiry and can act as a means of galvanising a change in practice. Historically, there have been various views on the role of HEI academics in this context, ranging from the notion of bringing rigour to school-based decisions (Hargreaves, 1996) to, more recently, the consideration of research as a means of addressing the disenfranchisement of teachers, where teachers are challenged to develop their own body of locally held knowledge (Coleman, 2007; Ebbut, Worrall and Robson, 2000). In the words of Louise Stoll (2009, p 125), it *boils down to creating a capacity for learning'*.

Beyond improving teaching and learning, evidence-based approaches can have wider positive ramifications. Nelson and O'Beirne (2014) suggest that teacher research can encourage teachers to work together more collegially, promote a proper focus on how to analyse and use existing school data, and help to build wider confidence as part of professional development. In turn teachers learn how to make informed choices about practice and use empirical data to cope with future change agendas. Teacher inquiry, if deployed school-wide, can become greater than the sum of its parts and can help to foster a professional learning community (PLC) (Harris, 2014). Teachers learn how to evaluate and critique their own practice and that of others to help them make informed choices. The role of the HEI academic as partner, coach, mentor or 'objective other' can help to maintain the focus on learning for everyone and to direct teacher reflections on practice. In turn, and with increased levels of confidence, teachers themselves can take on the role of consultants, advisors and critical friends. They can begin to challenge their own commonly held practices, develop their own discourses and reconceptualise their practice.

The advent of the new curriculum (Department for Education 2013, updated 2014) required students to engage more fully with 'deep thinking'. Those processes were best expedited by teachers, but in order to understand how to engage more critically with knowledge, many teachers may find it beneficial to have some theoretical concepts on hand in order to make greater sense of their practice (Postholm, 2009). The construction of a 'theory toolkit' can help to inform inquiry practices, particularly those related to choices of methodological approach.

Third spaces (crossing boundaries) to undertake research

Work intensification and the general busyness of primary schools may be a detractor for teachers to even begin to engage with EBT approaches. Coupled with demands from the inspectorate, the creation of a research culture in the primary school can only succeed if there is a strategic leadership vision to move the school from research-interested to research-engaged. Newly qualified teachers and those in challenging schools may feel 'vulnerable', constrained by the inspection framework and a lack of confidence around taking risks or being creative in their pedagogy. School leaders have to be prepared to take a leap of faith in order to allow their staff to see beyond their own classroom walls – what is known as working in the interstices between classroom and wider school structures. This is also known as 'boundary crossing'. Sometimes boundaries can be seen as barriers or sources of difficulty; or they can be regarded as opportunities for change and renewal. The idea is that teachers begin to inhabit a 'third space' (Bhabha, 1994) or cross a boundary. This might be a space on the agenda of a school staff meeting for a presentation, or critical dialogue about a particular subject led by a member of the teaching staff. The formal spaces to allow teachers to have a platform to disseminate their inquiry findings, for example, also provide learning spaces for teachers and contribute to ongoing professional development (Skattebol and Arthur, 2014). Outside these more formal structures, there can exist informal ones with the creation of networks where teachers work together on their inquiries. The legitimisation of inquiry as routine classroom practice that is fully supported by school leadership gives teachers the opportunity to disengage with tried-and-tested (and often faulty) pedagogical approaches and to re-engage with professional practice in ways that allow them to think more deeply about their pedagogy in a critical, increasingly objective way.

The creation of a third space with other inquiry-focussed colleagues assists the development of a body of knowledge around subject and pedagogical discourses that can be widely shared among professional staff. Having space to focus on teaching and learning with the express support of the leadership team creates a learning culture for both students and staff with:

the potential of creating such spaces for teaching and learning where children had as much right and opportunity as teachers to shape the agenda for learning and where teachers took risk in order to enhance pedagogy, how they calculated those risks and how they overcame related uncertainties to move forward in the efficacy of their practice.

(Broadhead, 2010, p 42)

This third space in turn becomes a repository for inquiry-focussed teachers to develop a body of knowledge around a subject and promotes pedagogical discourses that can be shared with all staff in other formal spaces. Orland-Barak (2009) points out that teachers have, over recent years, developed an 'answerism' approach to their practice, where they are charged with having to immediately respond with a solution to the problem.

Evidence-based inquiry helps to change that 'right answerism' approach and should, over time, help to create a self-sustaining community of professionals who not only regularly examine and critique their own practice but also share the outcomes of their work.

But in this school setting, before our teachers could inhabit a third space, we had to consider how best to get them interested in EBT; otherwise this project would be a non-starter. Val had always maintained that she, together with the head and the senior leadership team (SLT), were the best advocates for EBT and so decided to undertake her own research with the SLT to gain their perspectives as they trialled their own inquiries. She felt her role as 'guide on the side' as opposed to 'sage on the stage' (as had been the case in the workshop referred to above) would be the best approach.

Role-modelling research

The head and staff needed time to understand the implementation and processes of EBT. Even after the initial workshop given by Val, with support from Jon, many teachers were still very unsure of the whole process. For EBT to become a driver for a change in school culture, it was necessary to work with the SLT in order for them to understand and demonstrate the benefits of EBT to other teachers. Because they all had teaching roles, they had to become conversant in EBT processes and be prepared to role-model their practice to other teachers through a more open classroom approach. Val decided to conduct a small pilot study with the leadership team to gain a better understanding of how they perceived EBT and what they had learnt from it. This pilot research was conducted throughout the first year of the project, and a qualitative approach was adopted, involving the interviewing of the assistant heads after their initial engagement with EBT processes. Through engaging as participants with this research, they were able to reflect on their own teaching, and Val began to see them reconceptualise their own practice:

As a teacher graded outstanding by Ofsted I had become quite stale ... I requested an observation from the school improvement officer ... with a Year 6 class ... he said the learners were receptive but they didn't take control of their own learning ... not able to apply their learning. We talked about the Shanghai method of mastery ... I went away and read about it ... and then used it for my inquiry.

(interview with assistant headteacher 1)

It became clear that Val's role as supporter for inquiry and her vision for its dissemination would have to be ongoing, at least in the early stages of the project. It was clear that the language of academic research would have to be in some part 'translated' so that teachers were able to collect and analyse their data and design some form of dissemination. Most SLT members adopted an action-research approach to their inquiries, in the form of planning, doing, analysing and evaluating/reflecting. (Jennie discusses this in more detail in Chapter 3.) There were many learning points along the way for everyone participating in this venture, and so the pilot study became a piece of research that was shared within the school, at a subsequent conference in 2015 (Teacher Education Advancement Network) and published at a later date (Poultney, 2016). It became a way of mobilising the SLT into realising that their everyday professional practice could in fact be researched:

When you (Val) came into talk to us I was a bit like 'whoa!', this is massive, this is huge … then we discussed it a bit more … it was everyday things we do all the time … you don't think of it in an inquiry way.

(interview with assistant headteacher 2)

As work on individual inquiries continued, classroom and corridor displays began to demonstrate how teachers and children were engaging with EBT. Dissemination can take various forms: written, spoken and visual. Constructing displays is familiar territory to a primary school teacher and easily one of the most favoured ways of getting research messages out to other staff, children and parents. Visual evidence of this nature was also utilised as a means of recording the ongoing projects, and this was displayed outside the staffroom. More formally, teachers also populated their 'space' on the staff meeting agenda which became a weekly slot for the dissemination of the outcomes of their inquiries and a regular opportunity to debate and discuss next steps. This was an important factor in building teacher confidence around research, and it became clear that the school was becoming a smaller place as teachers liaised with each other as they shared outcomes of their practice from Foundation Stage to Year 6.

The effectiveness of internal dissemination was immediately obvious, and it was clear that this work had the potential to go external. This became a role that Jon (headteacher) was very keen to take on. In addition, one of the assistant headteachers was seeing the opportunities afforded to her by disseminating the findings more widely:

I needed something from my own classroom first of all to do the research but then I asked for this observation for some new ideas because within school we only know what we know … the best practitioners who have tried things and they say 'that works' – have a go at that. It would be nice to share things further, out at other schools. Maybe with the Academy Trust.

(assistant headteacher 3)

What we were beginning to see was a move towards the teachers developing their practice jointly (often termed joint practice development or JPD) and some movement towards a PLC. However, developments such as these do not happen overnight, nor does each and every member of staff engage or come along at the same rate. Some of the SLT were keen to disseminate their work as widely as possible and looked for opportunities at local and national meetings and conferences in line with their leadership roles. Other teachers were less inclined to do this in person, preferring to give a written account of their work. Some were keen to do both and to invite teachers from other schools to see the evidence of their change in practice. The important message here is that dissemination must be regarded as an integral part of teacher inquiry if teachers are to be engaged with it. It is part and parcel of the whole-school culture change and a means of documenting knowledge production. However, we were still grappling with what counted as quality evidence for research in the primary school. How useful were the data generated? Were these data measurable? Did these data evidence impact on learning?

What evidence constitutes effective research in school contexts?

One of the main challenges to teacher inquiry through use of evidence-based approaches has been around the quality of the outcomes of the research and what counts as robust evidence. Teachers are often dismissive of academic educational research as being unfit for their practice, and while government education policy is not consistently founded on the outcomes of academic research, teachers may have a point. The work of teachers is different from that of researching academics in terms of context, the means to be able to research, funding and having time to research. For the working professional, their research is necessarily based on inquiring into their own practice and is very much a subjective endeavour. It is usually aimed at addressing and improving a problem situation and is predicated on providing evidence that helps to solve that problem. For teachers who are interested, considering the outcomes of such inquiries gives them the opportunity to engage in critical conversations with other teachers about the findings, but rarely are such findings made public. The case studies written by teachers in this book may, on first reading, seem to produce only flimsy evidence and would in no way stand up to academic scrutiny. Teachers make sense of their practice by socially constructing their view of reality; they each hold different values about education, and the knowledge they produce from their inquiries is highly contextualised and difficult to replicate. Yet Jennie, Helen, Alison and Jacqui (the teachers writing for this book) have all been able to disseminate their findings in a variety of local and national contexts, and on no occasion did they fail to reach and engage their audience. Why? Because they had confidence in their findings. They did not present their research outcomes as 'proof', but they had data that other professionals recognised as valid within a primary school classroom and, perhaps more importantly, they could see the potential of the findings in their own individual settings.

Much of the evidence detailed in each case study following Chapter 2 may not look like academic data as we might understand it in more conventional research. We must remember that these inquiries were undertaken at a particular time, with a particular class of children and over a short time span, in most cases just one week. The common approach to gathering data was action research; thinking about things that puzzled teachers in their work, what they wanted to find out and why, and what type of intervention they could use to kick-start the research process. Outcomes of the research included interview transcripts from which teachers drew quotations (especially from children), assessment evidence, behaviour changes and improvement in children's spoken and written language. Jennie, Helen, Alison and Jacqui have all seen their work as a means of professional experiential learning that has enabled them to have licence to make changes to their teaching and learning practices (Foreman-Peck and Murray, 2009). Their work to date has been largely reserved for their own professional community where they feel more grounded and safe to evaluate their work with their professional peers. In this sense, the case studies presented in the following chapters represent what has worked for these teachers; but it has also enabled them to have a voice in school and be part of an emerging democratic environment.

The teachers all acknowledge the limitations of their inquiries and make no claim for true research authenticity. EBT approaches might not be a perfect approach to educational research (Biesta, 2007), but within the limits of what is possible for teachers to achieve in evaluating their practice, it seems to do 'what it says on the tin'.

Finally one of the issues left to resolve in research terms has been that of research ethics which, to date, teachers have only just begun to recognise. Because teaching is largely a moral endeavour (Oancea and Pring, 2009), teachers often feel that their professional code of ethics, teaching standards and qualified teacher status precludes them from addressing research ethics head on. This issue is very much part of future discussions as teachers move onto different forms of data collection and their knowledge of research grows. This is where the support given by an HEI academic can help to foster future research and the bid-writing opportunities that may subsequently arise and which Jon is keen in the future to follow up on. When considering what is educationally desirable, and the extent to which teacher-driven evidence exerts influence on wider school policy and beyond, there is another issue to take into account, namely the realisation that EBT approaches have the power to break long-held notions regarding pupil failure and that this itself can be a major factor in both raising standards and improving the educational landscape outlook for all.

Opportunities and challenges to EBT approaches

As the year progressed, I began to notice an increasing confidence in the researching teachers as they shared their outcomes in their groups. At the beginning of this project, it was not possible to foresee how the outcomes of EBT would impact on raising standards or how this work would influence a change in school culture that could be assessed as a change for the better. There were no blueprints for implementing this work, save for some academic accounts of how EBT had been implemented in primary schools elsewhere. Nor was it possible to understand how researching teachers would themselves cope with becoming more inquiry-focussed; so we asked the following questions:

» Would teachers gain more confidence in their work or would inquiry negatively destabilise their confidence?

» Would this 'third space' become too contested, too challenging an arena for the leadership team?

» Would teachers have to agree to research only certain areas of their practice, or could they be more autonomous about making such choices?

Jon had to be aware that an accumulation of research knowledge by his teaching team might pose a challenge to his own accountability systems and to the competing political agendas that shape current educational practice. At the beginning of this work, we took a 'leap of faith' regarding these issues and certainly did not consider them in depth.

Reflection points

»   We saw teachers gain confidence as a result of engaging with EBT. They used some of their new knowledge as power to challenge school leadership. Are school leaders confident and prepared for any challenges to their leadership style?

»   In your own school, would there be some research that you might welcome and other types of research you might discourage? How will you agree this with your staff?

Opportunities and challenges to undertaking teacher inquiry

It is important to stress that the climate for change must come from the headteacher and the SLT, and the school leaders need to understand how far this type of work may go in order to promote healthy two-way debate and positive disagreement and conflict. School leaders also need to be aware of times when this type of endeavour may promote just the opposite. Micropolitical issues cannot be ignored and may, in fact, prompt more staff to engage in research that results in a degree of challenge to current leadership orthodoxy. This aspect of teacher inquiry needs to be acknowledged as part of the change process.

We have drawn together in Table 1.1 some of the opportunities and challenges to EBT, but it is not a complete list. Different schools in different contexts will experience different opportunities and challenges, and leadership teams have to be prepared to celebrate the opportunities and to embrace the challenges, especially when initialising EBT across the school.

Table 1.1 gives a list of some of the main issues which may face schools undertaking teacher inquiry for the first time.

IN A **NUTSHELL**

Evidence-based teaching can impact positively on teacher practice and professional development. It can generate school knowledge that improves children's learning, energise and enthuse teachers and challenge school leaders in equal measure. Over time it can be a force for positive change in school culture.

Table 1.1 Opportunities and challenges of undertaking teacher inquiry

Opportunities	Challenges
Ongoing professional development that can be differentiated across a range of ages/expertise	Leaders must provide opportunities for teachers to engage in inquiry
Building confidence, improving teacher competence	Challenge to leadership decisions based on evidence collected through teacher inquiry
Developing teacher leadership; teachers have authority to become part of decision-making processes	Resourcing and structuring; providing the architecture for shift to EBT culture
Dissemination within and external to school	Appropriacy of setting performance-management targets for teachers based on their inquiry work
Raising standards of teaching and learning	Strategy for leading and managing inquiry across the school
Can-do approach to problem solving; professional ownership of solutions, risk-taking	Building a democratic inquiry process and managing the demands of accountability
Children, parents, support staff and governors can be involved in the work	Sustaining inquiry over a period of time to evidence impact on standards
Career development/promotion	Supporting teachers through inquiry including competency issues
Opportunities for initial teacher education (ITE) students to see research happening in primary classrooms	Being clear on how partnership between school and HEI academic will work in practice, over time and how to cope with change
Success and failure equally valued for the learning opportunities gained in the spirit of 'no one judged'	Widening the opportunities for teachers to take work outside of school: meetings, conferences

REFLECTIONS ON **CRITICAL ISSUES**

This chapter outlines some of the key issues for consideration when taking on a whole-school approach to EBT or teacher inquiry. There has to be good reason for its adoption and it must be thought through and carefully planned wherever possible. We have reflected on some of the important areas for introducing EBT from 'scratch' and offered our advice on this matter. We hope this chapter will provide some insights into the challenges that EBT brings and how, in preparation, leadership teams can begin to see the value of their continued role in EBT approaches and, importantly, how the value of EBT can be judged over time.

The following chapters outline the approach Allenton Community Primary School in Derby took towards embracing a culture of teacher inquiry. In Chapter 2 Val and Jon write about their experience of working together in a school–university partnership. In Chapters 3–5 Jennie, Helen, Alison and Jacqui recall their own experiences of EBT and reflect on what they have learnt. In Chapter 6 Jon reflects on how EBT was used to change school culture, and Val summarises the key points of learning in Chapter 7. Thank you for reading about our experiences. We hope you take at least one thing from this book that will help you in changing your own practice.

CHAPTER 2 | LEADING PRIMARY SCHOOL INQUIRY: WHAT DO WE NEED TO KNOW ABOUT SCHOOL–UNIVERSITY PARTNERSHIPS AND WAYS OF WORKING?

Val Poultney and Jon Fordham

CRITICAL **ISSUES**

- *Establishing a school–university relationship focussed on teacher research;*
- *Developing a reciprocal leadership relationship between headteacher and academic;*
- *Engaging school teachers and teacher educators in practitioner research agendas;*
- *Using research to inform how schools and Initial Teacher Education (ITE) departments understand evidence-based teaching.*

Introduction

This chapter focuses on how Jon, the headteacher, and Val, the university academic, worked together to lead the school from a research-interested to a research-engaged position. Through a growing partnership between the school and the university, this chapter examines how we endeavoured to make sense of our respective roles and different identities and the ways this has helped to change teaching and learning practice at Allenton Community Primary School. We discuss how we came to understand how best to lead research into professional practice, making it a central part of teacher learning and embedding it as a normal part of teachers' work. We describe a pilot year of study during which we experienced the highs and lows of implementing this research vision from initial failure to engage with teachers through to the same teachers writing for this publication. This chapter is an account of leadership work which offers some insights and reflections into the knowledge gained about how to approach, introduce and support research in a primary school.

Historical context of the school: taking a leap of faith

Allenton Primary is an inner city school located in Derby in the East Midlands of England, with over 70 per cent of children designated 'pupil premium' and high instances of pupil mobility. Pupil premium refers to the additional funding that schools receive to raise the attainment of disadvantaged pupils whatever their ability and to reduce any learning gaps between them and their peers. The school has academy status, and data returns indicate outcomes are generally below the national average. This somewhat chequered history has not helped the reputation of the school, yet staff are passionate about helping the children to achieve and many have remained working at the school for many years. The headteacher, Jon, is a relative newcomer to the school having secured headship just two years ago. At the time of this work in 2014–15, Jon was supported by a seconded deputy head and three assistant heads, all relatively new to the post. Jon was very keen to bring new ideas and initiatives into school to improve the quality of learning and teaching but had few means of critically evaluating the impact of individual class projects beyond simple school data progress indicators.

Reflection point

»   Think about a current practice which you feel has been working well in your school or partner school. What evidence might you gather to support your positive perspective?

Our developing partnership allowed us to evaluate some recently introduced school practices such as 'non-negotiables' which were mainly classroom routines Jon had asked teachers to adopt in order to bring some consistency to teaching approaches across the whole school. Jon had consulted the NFER *Self-Review Tool for Research Engagement in Schools* (2015) which advised school leaders to collaborate with research partners and to build a research environment in school which engaged staff in research and inquiry. The advice also suggested building external networks to sustain the research momentum going forward. We both felt this early evaluation of 'where we are now' was a good benchmark from where we could begin to engage with teacher research. There were few structures in place to support this type of work or the academic capacity with which to engage the staff in the inquiry work. The next challenge was to consider our next steps and the direction of our own professional relationship.

Reflection point

»   Consider auditing the current research capacity in your school or partner school. Staff with, or those studying for, higher degrees will probably have some research knowledge. Who might provide additional peer support to help develop school-based research? You might want to look at the 'Research-engaged school health check' diagnostic tool available from NCSL accessed via www.silkalliance.org.uk/docs/r&d/Leading_a_research_engaged_school.pdf, page 18.

Working beyond the professional boundaries

While Jon and I might have been very convinced of the worth of practitioner inquiry to improve standards and secure better outcomes for children, we were unsure strategically of how to introduce the idea to staff. Drawing on the literature (Skattebol and Arthur, 2014; Ainscow et al, 2016), we were reminded that there were potentially many pitfalls, especially in the early stages of selling the initiative to staff and maintaining the research momentum. Jon was sure about one thing – he wanted to change the school culture to a researching one. We did not at this stage envisage a celebratory outcome for our work as suggested by Mockler and Groundwater-Smith (2015), but we adopted a positive approach and agreed that learning from our mistakes could be just as valuable. In those early stages we were building:

- » trust (with each other and between school and university);

- » respect (for each other's position in school and university);

- » reciprocal professional working relationships (with school leaders and staff);

- » clarity of communication (between Jon and Val; and Jon, senior leadership team (SLT) and teaching staff);

- » understanding of research methodologies (as appropriate to researching practitioners).

We agreed that this work would take staff beyond the normal 'one-day course' and the passing-on of technical knowledge. This approach had previously made little impact on teachers changing their pedagogy and had therefore failed to drive up standards. The very fact that the school was seen as 'challenging' gave us the authority to take some leadership risks, but we agreed that this type of work needed time, some 'safe spaces' where teachers could research into their own practice and have the opportunity to disseminate their outcomes. For Val, a recent Ofsted inspection into Initial Teacher Education (ITE) at the university had commented positively on university staff supporting evidence-based teaching (EBT) approaches in challenging schools, and the Carter Review (2015) had similarly flagged this as an important part of trainee teachers' learning. This, coupled with Jon's full commitment to the project, meant that we were ready to start engaging with the wider school staff. Val agreed to conduct a workshop with the staff where she explained the rationale for this approach and some basic supporting theory, and invited staff to discuss how some of their current work could be researched. As noted in Chapter 1, the staff were polite but relatively unenthusiastic about adopting such an approach, although they agreed the session was interesting. We were disappointed by the reaction of staff to the workshop but began to understand that we needed another way of convincing them of the worth of EBT. We agreed that Jon needed to demonstrate how to be a researching professional so that teachers could see an example of how EBT works in practice.

Role-modelling practitioner research

We learnt from the workshop that if we were asking teachers to undertake their own research, then not only did we need to support them but we also had to role-model the research process as well. Many of Jon's new initiatives to embed some whole-school routines were possible foci for some evaluation research; we agreed that he would conduct some research into 'DIRT' (Dedicated Improvement Reflection Time), a five-minute reflection conducted at the beginning of every lesson by all teachers. Jon felt the best way to capture these types of data was by use of video, and he therefore spent one week filming these short sessions. In our next meeting, we reflected on the quality of the data, and Jon began to understand the difficulties of video that fails to adequately capture teacher and pupil responses. The data were almost meaningless, but the meeting gave us space to consider alternative methodologies, and a new approach was adopted, involving the use of a questionnaire and follow-up interviews to collect data. Findings revealed not only what was taking place in classrooms but other issues related to levels of literacy and numeracy, and most importantly provided a basis for some further teacher discussions.

Reflections on our approach to teacher research

Reflecting on all of this, we concluded that teachers do not need to understand research methodologies in detail but benefit from advice from an HEI academic as to the best research approaches. There is a need to think about the boundary between what you consider to be 'normal professional practice' and 'research'. In particular, we discussed some of the ethical implications for staff and children taking part in research of this type and how we could deal with this issue.

> » Think about and discuss the most appropriate methodology for research.
>
> » Allow mistakes to happen – they are great learning platforms.
>
> » Begin to identify staff who are able to act as an advocate for research approaches.
>
> » Put practitioner research matters on the staff meeting agenda.
>
> » Disseminate all research outcomes on a display board near the staffroom.
>
> » Start talking and using research outcomes from professional and academic sources.

Reciprocal leadership: mutual approaches to leading and supporting EBT

Much of the research about the working relationship between a head and an academic is built on anecdotes, small case studies where lessons have been learnt and are often reported post-relationship (Beckett, 2016). It is often described from an academic's perspective rather than a head's; so using our combined knowledge of leadership and research, we decided to undertake our own research into embedding EBT with the wider leadership team. The deputy head was leaving the school to take up a headship; so we focussed on the three assistant headteachers who had agreed to undertake some of their own EBT work following Jon's role-modelling exercise with the DIRT initiative. Two of the assistant heads, Jennie and Helen, report on their work in Chapters 3 and 4.

Jon's role-modelling approach had the impact of giving staff confidence to try out some EBT approaches in their own classrooms. We had agreed that this work should not, at this stage, be any part of performance management, nor should any members of staff be forced into participating with this approach. The assistant heads had agreed they would 'road-test' some of the EBT approaches and for different reasons: Helen was looking for ways in which to extend the writing of Year 6; and Jennie was actively trying to push up the levels of writing needed as evidence for the 'Big Write', a whole-school approach to raising stand-ards in writing; Sharon was interested in transition issues from Foundation Stage to Year 1 and was gathering evidence to better understand some of the challenges children faced as they entered Year 1. Jon made EBT an agenda item for the staff meeting and requested assistant heads report on their progress, and a display board outside the staffroom was designated as an information board about all matters to do with EBT and research in general. A journal club was initiated as another means of opening up discussion about new initiatives and research papers, and Val gained ethical approval to run an evaluation of the EBT pilot year (Poultney, 2016) which would record the perspectives from the assistant heads and Jon over the next year. Val was invited to join the Derby Teaching Schools Alliance (DTSA) Strategic Advisory Board so that she could help develop the research and development strand of 'Big 6' (part of the government's drive to give schools the freedom to take responsibility for managing their own school systems; research and development is sixth on this list of criteria) and get the work of Allenton out to a wider external audience.

Reflection points

» Start small; think big. If you are a university academic, become part of teacher networks and consider researching with the school leadership team to improve your own personal and professional credibility with them.

» Look for as many ways as possible to embed EBT in a school: a few small changes can make a lot of difference to building teachers' confidence.

Sustaining the school–university relationship over time

The first year of our work was a most intense time as we strived to keep EBT high on eve-ryone's agenda. We kept in regular contact through school and DTSA meetings, email and telephone. We played to our own strengths and contacts; Jon saw opportunities through his professional contacts, and I considered ways in which the school could get the EBT work out to academic and professional audiences. I also saw the opportunity to bring EBT to other schools in our ITE partnership in similar circumstances so that we could build a cadre of researching schools. The take-up of the EBT approach by other local primaries was patchy, with various reasons ranging from not being 'ready' for this type of work through to being 'too busy' (usually prefaced with 'in preparation for Ofsted'). Most successes were achieved using one of the Allenton assistant heads as 'EBT Advocate' who would deliver a session with staff promoting the opportunities of engaging with EBT, followed up by a visit from Val to explain more about the possible methodologies teachers could use. We found this joint approach very successful, and it was well-received at a recent heads' conference (Fordham et al, 2015). This approach is very much in line with Sebba, Kent and Treganza's (2012) view of 'Joint Professional Development' but carried out initially within school and then later building networks with other schools. Additionally we have been working to populate the DTSA's own research and development strand, but the impact of such work is slow, given much of the Teaching School Alliance (TSA) courses are predicted on training (the one-day-course approach) rather than a more sustainable model of school improvement. This point has been observed elsewhere (Ainscow et al, 2016, p 18), where it was noted that knowledge transfer between TSAs is akin to the old local authority model of delivering 'training':

Whatever the explanation, the disappointment for us is that effective strategies based on practitioner inquiry are less evident within the programmes offered by the new teaching schools. The predominant model involves training activities that present practice as being mainly about the passing on of technical knowledge, rather than as an activity that involves 'joint practice development' of the sort that is widely endorsed by research evidence.

We would argue that, in line with Hargreaves and Fullan (2012), schools have to be encouraged to build academic and decisional capacity so that they have their own locally researched knowledge. We would also suggest that in schools such as Allenton where achieving the high test scores measured by national tests is a constant challenge, there is the space for EBT to develop so that teachers become highly skilled at adapting to new approaches to teaching. This would seem to fit with James and Oplatka's (2015) view of the 'good enough' school, a term coined by Winnicott in 1953. The school does not offer a 'model of good practice' that can be packaged up and used by other schools; the challenge for us is convincing others that there are necessary steps to take in school as part of preparing teachers to change their mindset from a training to an EBT approach. Part of the school–university relationship has been one of some success because we each draw upon our respective school and university experiences and expertise, but our challenge has been around engaging with theory only accessible if teachers are registered students of the university. Teachers who are not students at the university have no access to academic literature beyond what is available on, for example, Google Scholar and other websites. Due to copyright issues, I (as university academic) was unable to share relevant journal articles with teachers that were not freely available on the web. We came to an arrangement with the university library to allow teachers who were not registered students of the university to borrow up to five books, which would help them gauge a broader theoretical understanding of their practice.

Reflection points

» Is there a collective vision for leading learning in your school/partnership school?

» What is it and what strengths does each leader bring in order to achieve that vision?

Researching with SLT

Jon had already undertaken some inquiry research into one of his own initiatives by way of role-modelling research, but we felt more credibility for research can be gained if staff could see the leadership team engaging with it themselves. This credibility also extended to the HEI academic who felt personally that in addition to showcasing (or role-modelling) research methodologies it might be useful to take stock of senior leaders' perceptions of EBT as practice. This would allow us to have a form of benchmarking so that further research with the team could be done, but based on evidence. It might also allow us to use the outcomes of the research to present to external professional and academic audiences with the possibility of a future publication (Poultney, 2016). After much discussion, we decided that this would be a piece of research carried out as part of the pilot year. There were four aims of the research:

1. how to introduce teacher inquiry (roles of head and HEI academic);

2. how to lead teacher inquiry (by whom, how and when);

3. how to sustain teacher inquiry (what support is needed);

4. what lessons can the school and academy (university) learn from this work?

The research approach was essentially a sequential mixed-methods study that sought the views and perspectives of the SLT comprising the headteacher and his three assistant headteachers. Each participant completed a short Likert-style questionnaire followed up by a longer, one-hour, in-depth, semi-structured interview.

Findings of the pilot research

The findings of this pilot research revealed that, while most of the leaders were positive about conducting their own inquiries, there were some issues for which they needed more support. These included:

» a point of contact who could help them reach a clear focus for inquiry and related specific research questions;

» how to work ethically;

» how to make sense of their data.

They were surprised to find that they all related this work back to their own initial teacher training and further reflected that professionally they did not regularly revisit those research skills they had learnt as trainees. Collectively they had, to some extent, dismissed theory in favour of practice – 'tips for teaching' had overridden their need to engage with their own or published research. They had failed to relate to the theory presented in Val's workshop, yet they agreed in carrying out their own pieces of research that they now felt more confident about engaging with published research. They had not seen themselves as leaders of learning except within their own classrooms; they had not shared their work nor seen a reason for any dissemination. They had rarely questioned their own practice, and some were reluctant to make any changes to practice on the say-so of an HEI academic.

There was a certain type of vulnerability about this group of school leaders in the way they engaged with Val's research, a point noted by McIntyre and Hobson (2015) in their research with early-career teachers. The constraints of the profession, the inspection framework and the 'culture of compliance', observed by Hargreaves as far back as 1994, was not allowing these leaders to create the space they needed in order to examine their own and others' practice. Another outcome of the research showed that leaders valued EBT as the vehicle to bring them together socially, a legitimisation to discuss all matters related to teaching and learning. The link with Val therefore began to be seen as a more legitimate relationship, especially as teachers were also supported formally in writing up their research and understanding methodological approaches, and informally through regular meetings and Val dropping by at school to see research progress. The spirit of our work became 'everyone researching', and this pilot research became integral in not only engaging staff in research but also allowing Val to 'activate the hyphen' around the 'insider-outsider' research position that she held (Broadhead, 2010, p 41) within the school and as a researching academic.

The difficult time in convincing the SLT of the benefits of teacher inquiry was somewhat ameliorated when one or two initiatives, brought into school by Jon, were evaluated in classrooms and positive outcomes were evidenced. Peer critique, discussed by Jennie in Chapter 3, was a resounding success in Year 6 and especially with the 'Big Write' approach, something which lower attaining children regularly had difficulty completing. Val began to notice that many display boards in class and in the corridors were showing evidence of how children had engaged with peer critique (EL Education, 2012). Further, this evidence was appearing from Foundation Stage through Key Stage 1 and into Key Stage 2 up to Year 6. The SLT reported that, along with this visual evidence, regular dissemination at weekly staff meetings was encouraging teachers to engage with this initiative. One of the assistant heads was actively researching and collecting an evidence base on peer critique; it was an example of how this initiative had caught the imagination of a range of teachers.

Reflection point

> »   Think about what gives licence for teachers to undertake any form of research in school. How is research supported and resourced? What role does the academic take in all of this?

Dissemination of EBT

The success of this work could be measured in many ways, but for us the main drivers centred on raising standards. Val had been clear from the outset that dissemination, in various forms, was also an integral part of the work and her role was important in leading Jon and the SLT in promoting this course of action.

» In the beginning, EBT progress was reported as a standing agenda item in the weekly staff meetings. This gave opportunity for all staff including NQTs, RQTs and trainees to take part. It helped to build confidence and provide a safe space for critical reflection of practice. Val had decided not to attend these meetings so that a measure of independence could be fostered by the staff.

» As a result of Jon's many meetings with DTSA, the academy trust, the journal club and other professional encounters, visits of staff from other schools in the academy were made and the outcomes of the work shared more widely across the schools.

» Jon was keen to be part of an academic audience, and a paper was presented at the Teacher Education Advancement Network (TEAN) in May 2015.

» Val and others continued to disseminate the work at academic conferences, for example, TEAN (Fordham and Poultney, 2015); teaching and learning conference, University of Derby (Poultney, 2015); headteachers' conference, DTSA (Fordham et al, 2015).

» Meantime, work had taken place with other local primary schools that had also taken on the teacher inquiry approach and was being used as part of teaching for BEd students engaging with their dissertation research.

At the end of the pilot year, Val organised an 'away-day' at the university where teachers were given the opportunity to disseminate their work to a range of professional and academic staff, many of whom were not Allenton staff. We were very surprised to find two teachers, Jacqui and Alison – who had never been seen to engage with EBT or disseminate it with colleagues in school – present their research at this event. They had simply worked quietly and out of sight until they felt it was the right time to share their work. Their work is presented in Chapter 5.

Reflection points

» Share your research outcomes with as many professionals as is possible. What opportunities arise for different school-based teachers to engage with the local HEI and work with trainee teachers? Could your work be of interest within your own partnership or as part of a professional or academic conference?

» Consider how to celebrate the outcomes of work achieved as part of teacher research and how you can provide alternative ways for teachers to disseminate their work. Could the work be presented to ITE students in the university by school staff?

» How successful might you be initiating teacher research in school if you force everyone to engage with it? If this work is presented as a choice, then respect those teachers who do not immediately engage with the work. They may surprise you later on!

» The impact of EBT is not just confined to school. It is beginning to have impact in HEIs, encouraging some ITE staff to engage in their own research and to embed inquiry as practice into the undergraduate curriculum. What revisions could you make to your research-methods curriculum to reflect EBT approaches used by teacher researchers?

IN A **NUTSHELL**

Reciprocal leadership is a core component of a school–university partnership focussed on engaging everyone in building research capacity in a school and an ITE department.

REFLECTIONS ON **CRITICAL ISSUES**

Our work in engaging staff to undertake inquiry required us to work as leaders of learning. Our identities have changed as a result of this leadership relationship. We have worked reciprocally, and our assessment of our leadership 'value' is based on the successes, gains and lessons learnt in the context of professional learning. As an academic, Val has been aware of her role in this work as a leader of learning and ways in which she can embrace interconnectivity (between academy and schools, TSAs, other heads and academics) and sociocultural ways of being. The idea of this leadership relationship is grounded in a participatory leadership style, based on the notion of 'conscious leadership' (Jones and Brazdau, 2015). Both Jon and Val have experienced the uncertainties, opportunities and challenges of this leadership work as they move into each other's domains and try to make sense of their collective research. We are convinced that changing school culture from research-interested to research-engaged is about having a commitment to capacity building. Our leadership endeavours have taken the best part of two years of work; lessons have been learnt but the impact of the work continues. We are now seeing this work being led by other teachers as 'inquiry advocates' or 'horizon scanners' as the resources for inquiry are now well embedded as part of Allenton's culture. Our collective practice has been put under the microscope as leaders of learning and has provided a very powerful approach to changing both leadership and pedagogical practice.

CRITICAL ISSUES

- *Using peer critique as an approach to raise standards of writing;*
- *Aligning a piece of evidence-based teaching with new curriculum requirements for literacy;*
- *Engaging children in assessing and being responsible for their own work;*
- *Using peer critique as a strategy to encourage other teachers to engage with research into their own practice.*

Introduction

This chapter outlines the first whole-school initiative that was trialled and disseminated throughout the school. The role of the teacher as researcher is considered, and the evolution of the initiative from its beginning, the rationale for change and how it all worked in practice is discussed. The chapter outlines the impact of the initiative and how it was adapted to suit classes across the primary phase from Foundation Stage to Year 6. It discusses how the initiative was disseminated throughout the school to improve CPD (continuing professional development) and how evidence was used to inform whole-school policy and raise expectations around improving writing. The success of peer critique allowed teachers to engage with evidence-based teaching (EBT) as a powerful tool to raise standards while giving teachers back professional trust and responsibility for their teaching. Peer critique became a catalyst for change, empowering teachers to see how research could be used in the classroom and how they could share their good practice, thus making a contribution to real school improvement. This chapter features 'before and after' photographs of children's work. The quotes are derived from children and staff about the success of the trial.

Reflections on introducing EBT

Before Allenton Primary became an academy in 2015, the take-up of CPD courses on offer from the local authority was patchy with little strategic planning of professional development. As a school with significant weaknesses as identified by Ofsted in 2011, Allenton needed a way to improve the quality of its provision and to raise standards. In order to become a self-improving school, staff had to understand that they had to work together to improve teaching and learning. EBT was an approach that enabled staff to regain control over their own classroom practice. It provided a strategy that would benefit the children and be tailored to their specific needs. Over time, EBT restored teachers' trust in their own pro-fessionalism and empowered them to deliver lessons that would have the greatest impact on children's learning by matching the teaching to the specific needs of their children. The school's key priorities were linked to literacy and raising outcomes for all children. The new curriculum had a strong emphasis on editing and improving work, and this, combined with a need to raise standards in literacy, provided the school with a platform for an evidence-based project. Peer critique was a strategy for research suggested by the headteacher following a headteachers' network meeting and was initially introduced in Year 6 only.

What does peer critique look like?

Peer critique is based upon the work of Ron Berger (2003) and 'Austin's butterfly' (EL Education, 2012). Both sources aim to encourage children to be more reflective and inde-pendent learners so that they can identify next learning steps for themselves. As teachers we regularly give feedback to children on next steps and the targets they need to achieve for ongoing improvement. As a school, Allenton recognised that we needed to begin to empower our children so that they could reflect on their learning and take some ownership over the learning process. This extract from Berger (2003, p 8) reflects upon the trans-formative power of an individual piece of learning:

I believe that work of excellence is transformational. Once a student sees that he or she is capable of excellence, that student is never quite the same. There is a new self-image, a new notion of possibility. There is an appetite for excellence. After students have had a taste of excellence, they're never quite satisfied with less; they're always hungry. When the teachers at the Austine School for the Deaf pointed out to Sonia that many students wouldn't obsess over their work as she does, her reply was quick: This school has ruined me for life, she said. I'm never satisfied with anything until it's almost perfect. I have to be proud of it.

Teacher reflections

As part of classroom practice, verbal peer feedback was regularly used and children were frequently asked to explain to others something they liked and something that they thought could be done better. We had begun to recognise the power of peer critique and how by using it we could foster greater independence and reflectiveness among the children so that 'the most important assessment that goes on in a school isn't done to students but goes on inside students' (Berger, 2003, p 103), but we had failed to realise its full potential. Getting children to discuss their work with a peer worked quite well, and children were able to explain something they liked about each other's work in relation to the lesson objectives. Collectively we found that children often fell back on rather superficial things when sug-gesting improvements, for example, more factual information about quality of handwriting and spelling mistakes rather than the quality of the work. However, peer critique as an initiative seemed to be a way to take this peer support feedback to the next level and with a structure to help children become more specific when critiquing the work of others. This in turn meant that they had a greater understanding of what needed to be done to achieve a certain level and gave them a clearer sense of next-step goals that they could translate into their own work.

Implementation and impact of peer critique

Peer critique was initially introduced on a small scale into Year 6 by two of the assistant headteachers. As a senior leadership team (SLT) we were aware of the need to raise the quality of writing and the independence and reflectiveness of children; these were both key priorities on the school action plan, and peer critique was seen as a way to achieve both these key objectives. It was decided to introduce the strategy in Year 6 initially as this was where two members of the SLT were working, and the ability spread in the year group enabled us to see how the strategy could be used with a range of children before we asked other members of staff to trial it. Peer critique was trialled in both maths and literacy, across a range of abilities, to see how it could be adapted across subjects (as it naturally lends itself to literacy and writing). The initial introduction of peer critique began by showing the children the video of Austin's butterfly and discussing with them how the work was improved through listening to the advice of our peers and using our friends as guides. The video was a particularly powerful way of explaining to the children what peer critique was and they were motivated as they saw how pupils on the video suggested to Austin how he might improve his butterfly drawings. As a result of seeing the impact of the video, the children were keen to begin using the strategy as they could see how it could help them with their learning.

In maths, peer critique was trialled with higher-attaining children who, despite having a good grasp of basic numeracy, struggled with problem solving and the application of strategies in problems that required children to engage with high levels of literacy. With this group, the strategy was introduced by giving the children a maths problem and asking them to have a go at solving it with a partner. After ten minutes, the children paired up with another duo and shared how they had interpreted the problem and what they had done to solve it. The second pair then had to make a suggestion about the method they had used – they were encouraged to say something kind about what they had done, something specific about the method used and something helpful to enable the children to continue their working-out.

This worked well and the feedback from the children was really positive, with many saying it had given them a new idea that meant they could carry on the investigation longer. The children were very supportive of each other and were able to use the language of peer support. The feedback from a peer seemed to renew enthusiasm when problem solving and stopped the usual slump, when children get as far as they can but still have a long way to go. By stopping and critiquing each other's work, the children were much more successful at completing the task. Here are some of the quotes taken at the end of the lesson:

Peer support helped me improve my work. I hadn't thought about using brackets and they reminded me.

(child 1)

Peer support gave me new ideas when I was stuck.

(child 2)

In literacy, peer critique was trialled with higher- and lower-attaining children. Many of the lower-attaining children struggled with the language of peer support, and so in order to support these children, a proforma was created using the 'Be Kind, Be Specific, Be Helpful' prompts. However, the first time this was trialled it was evident that more support was needed in order to encourage the children to give more fulsome responses. It also seemed that more coaching on the appropriate types of response was needed! A proforma (Figure 3.1) was therefore devised which, while structuring the feedback, left it much more flexible for children's responses. For less able children, this was adapted to include only one of the sentences, as when trialled some children thought they needed to answer all statements rather than the most appropriate to what they wanted to say.

The children responded really well to this as it gave a structure for their feedback and guided those children who struggled to know how to phrase their responses. Following a piece of writing, they swapped work and gave feedback on each other's work, linked to the focussed targets set at the start of the session. The children were positive about the use of peer critique, but there were some social difficulties related to children's negative understanding of the word 'critique'.

Reflection point

» Many of the children in my group had self-esteem issues which meant they took any criticism in a negative way, at times becoming hostile and aggressive to their peers as they felt it meant their peers did not like them. This is something that needs careful consideration when implementing in the classroom, and pairings should be based on your knowledge of the class and how well they respond to each other.

The feedback from the first-round peer critique was then incorporated in a second draft of the children's work. They were asked to repeat the exercise with a different partner and then to complete a third draft. As each peer support session went on, the feedback became more focussed, and this meant a rise in almost a level for some children between the first and third drafts of their work. A level is a set of eight bands, set by government, to measure a child's progress compared with other children of the same age. These levels apply to children in Key Stage 1, Key Stage 2 in primary school and Key Stage 3 in secondary school. Many in the lower-attaining group struggled to stay focussed, and some became disheartened after the second draft which meant that the impact between second and final drafts was not as impressive as that between the first and second. Initially, a single revision worked better with lower-attaining children as they could see an improvement without

STAGE 4 PROMPT SHEET

Kind

I really like the way you _____

Excellent _____ throughout

The most successful thing about this was _____

I enjoyed reading this because _____

It was especially effective when _____

Specific

In the first / second / third paragraph...

I think _____ is quite difficult to understand / could be explained better / could include more detail etc.

Your sentence / paragraph about _____ was _____ because _____

To make progress you need to _____

Helpful (refer to success criteria)

Have you considered including _____

Think about taking away _____

Have you thought about _____

To improve your _____ try _____

Perhaps you could...? _____

Figure 3.1 Prompt sheet used in literacy

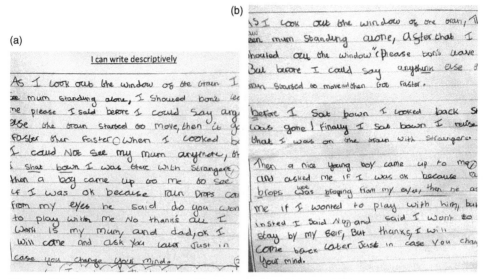

Figure 3.2 Example of improved writing for a lower-attaining child

becoming bored at repeating the same exercise. The impact of getting children to evaluate each other's work though was impressive and enabled many children to move from working in a level 2 to working at a level 3.

With the higher-attaining group, peer critique was used alongside the end-of-year expectations as well as specific targets for a lesson. As these children were more confident and had a greater understanding of literacy, their feedback and the language used was of a higher standard than that of the lower-attaining group, where targets needed to be modelled in more depth. Peer critique was used in a more advanced way with the higher attaining group with children looking through each other's work and highlighting three things they liked ('Be Kind') and three things to be improved ('Be Helpful'). When it came to the 'Be Specific' aspect, the children needed to identify where improvements could be made and then give examples such as 'In paragraph 2 you could add a simile such as…'.

What was the impact of the initiative?

Peer critique was quickly seen as a powerful tool for improving writing in Year 6. The children's work rapidly improved between the first and final drafts, and as the improvements were not ones suggested by a teacher, we were able to use the final piece of work as an assessed piece, rather than using the first draft as we had done previously. The successes in Year 6 were then shared with the rest of the staff in a whole-school staff session and the staff were given time to discuss the strategy and how it might work across school. They were then asked to trial peer critique for themselves and informed that this would be followed up in a subsequent staff session.

(a)

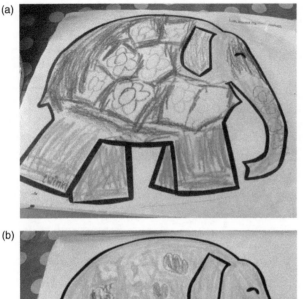

(b)

Figure 3.3 Before and after drawings completed by Foundation Stage pupil

Peer critique was quickly trialled in Foundation Stage through art/creative sessions, and the impact here was also significant as is shown in Figure 3.3.

Again children were listening to the advice of their peers and changing their own work, with significant improvements. Peer critique was also trialled with Year 2 and similar successes were reported. These success stories were shared with staff at the follow-up staff meeting where adopting the strategy across the whole school was discussed.

Reflection point

> » Think about what type of evidence you collect and use as data from your inquiry. In this case Jennie used a proforma, but in Foundation Stage Jayne collected and compared photographs of the children's work. Use these data to share the outcomes with a wider staff audience.

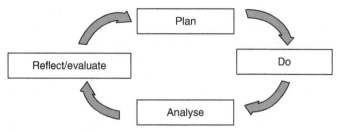

Figure 3.4 Action-research cycle

Action research

As part of the EBT approach, staff were asked to complete a simple reflection cycle, and this helped to formalise the initiatives being introduced and meant that the impact and outcomes were given high priority. The cycle contained four basic aspects and was not intended to be an onerous task but rather a tool to support and justify the initiatives being introduced. Figure 3.4 outlines this simple but effective action-research cycle.

When introduced to the action cycle as a model for data gathering, staff could begin to understand how to engage with teacher inquiry. I had provided data to evidence improvement in writing, so the impact was powerful and measurable which gave a good example of how peer critique could work in practice. Staff agreed that the use of peer critique could raise standards if implemented across the whole school. This decision was more readily agreed to, due to the trials we had conducted in Year 6, and data was beginning to show evidence of the positive outcomes. Peer critique was no longer seen as something that could only work in Year 6, and we had the opportunity to 'iron out' any issues before suggesting that the whole school should engage with the initiative.

As a school we recognised the significant impact that peer critique was having on pupil outcomes, but we needed to give significant consideration to the time required to do it properly as an initiative. Peer critique needs to be carefully managed in order to be successful. Time is needed for the children to create their first draft, and additional time is required for discussion/ peer critique of each other's work. Time needs to be allocated for improvements to take place and there should be a consideration of how many times the action cycle in Figure 3.4 will have to take place in order to evaluate the worth of any changes to teacher pedagogy.

Reflection point

» Consider how many times you need to go through the action-research cycle – once, twice or more – and the age/stage/phase of your children. Peer critique involves self-esteem issues for some children, and this is a judgement call for you as teacher to be aware of some of the negative impacts of the initiative.

On a whole-school level, the impact of introducing peer critique was extremely powerful. The ethos of the school altered and staff were able to see how they could use peer critique with their own classes. Staff became more collaborative in the way they were working and were keen to share their successes with other staff. There was a feeling that their opinions were listened to when creating whole-school changes (it was no longer something done to teachers but rather something they now had a voice in) and that they were once again trusted as professionals. This increased confidence led to staff developing their own EBT projects. Staff were keen to raise standards for children and now felt trusted to trial an idea in their teaching room that they believed would improve pupil outcomes and that might be shared and adopted as whole-school policy. For many of the staff, this change in ethos, brought about following a change in headteacher, was the first time they had been involved in decision-making and they felt empowered and trusted as professionals.

We decided, as a whole school, that we wanted to keep this momentum going and created manager roles to support the implementation of EBT across the school. Our journey for this can be seen in Figure 3.5.

Staff engaged with EBT as a strategy to raise standards, but some staff reported that it could be difficult to think of ideas/strategies to use in class. To provide further support, two new roles were created to help teachers devise initiatives that linked to the whole-school policy and to address issues arising from their own classrooms. The first role was the 'Horizon Scanner' who reviewed the school's action plan and, depending on the priorities, identified appropriate initiatives to help achieve school targets.

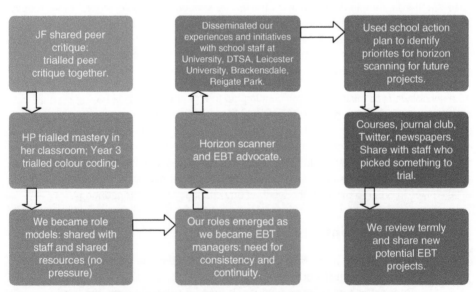

Figure 3.5 A flowchart to document stages in implementation of an EBT strategy

In addition they would also source any recent and relevant professional/academic research that related to this initiative that was then disseminated to staff. The second role was the 'EBT Advocate' who would trial these ideas in their own classroom and be able to offer practical support to teachers with their own projects. The creation of these EBT roles meant that there was an SLT investment in EBT and gave staff responsibility for the projects being run in school where they were expected to reflect on the impact of the strategies trialled. Staff were then required to link the strategies to the school's development plan and, should they encounter any difficulties, seek the advice of the EBT advocate as the 'go-to' person in school. For the school, EBT has been one of the most successful strategies for change and has led to staff having greater confidence and ownership over change while developing their reflectiveness as practitioners.

Ten things to consider when implementing peer critique as an approach to school improvement

1. What is the most effective way of explaining peer critique to the children?

2. How will you pair/group the children to undertake critique of each other's work? Who works well with each other? Are there other influences outside of school that may affect children's ability to work together? How will children cope with mixed attaining pairings?

3. Are there any self-esteem issues that need addressing before peer critique can be implemented?

4. How will you scaffold whole-school initiatives such as our 'Be Kind, Be Helpful, Be Specific' approach, which are fundamental to the principles of EBT, among children?

5. What support will the children need in making meaningful suggestions for improvement?

6. How many drafts/cycles of peer critique are your children able to manage without becoming disheartened and giving up?

7. How much time do you need to designate to peer critique as part of a unit of work?

8. What type of evidence/data will you collect and present to show improvement/ impact of the initiative?

9. How will you disseminate your outcomes and to whom?

10. Who are the 'go-to' people in school to discuss your inquiry work?

IN A **NUTSHELL**

Peer critique is an initiative which can be used to improve children's learning. It can also be a vehicle for teachers to become interested in researching and disseminating their changing practice. It empowers children through encouraging them to improve their work and that of their peers and can help to make them more reflective writers.

REFLECTIONS ON **CRITICAL ISSUES**

Inspired by the work of Berger (2003) and as a whole-school initiative to raise children's aspirations and levels of literacy, peer critique became a vehicle that engaged the hearts and minds of the children and teachers. Giving children 'licence' to verbalise their thoughts about their work and what they did not understand promoted their independence and improved their social skills and empathy with their peers. For the teachers, they realised that peer critique had potential in all subject areas and across the whole school from Foundation Stage to Year 6. It was an initiative that had everyone talking about their work – from the children about their learning to the teachers beginning to understand the possibilities of using peer critique with their class. Children's and teachers' confidence began to grow as they engaged with peer critique and, for the children, this confidence led to improved learning outcomes and attainment. For the teachers, they began to understand how to research and evidence good practice through an action-research approach and, importantly, how to disseminate their work with colleagues. Peer critique was one of the most successful pieces of EBT initiatives at Allenton and was, and is still today, a regular feature in classroom and corridor displays, children's work and teachers' marking and feedback.

CRITICAL **ISSUES**

- *Using active learning to improve learning behaviours in children;*
- *How varying pedagogy engages and enthuses learners;*
- *How to implement, plan and deliver active sessions;*
- *Working towards a complete culture change to focus on facilitating learning rather than teaching;*
- *How to disseminate the research outcomes to other staff.*

Introduction

This chapter outlines an initiative called active learning which was implemented by an experienced classroom practitioner and a newly qualified teacher. The chapter begins by giving a specific class context with a focus on how learning behaviours required some modification. The work follows a previous trial called 'Learning to Learn' and considers how these changes in approaches to learning were scaffolded by the teachers to improve the learning attitudes of children in a Year 6 class. This chapter explains how a range of active sessions were introduced to prepare children for learning. The use of social media (Twitter and Pinterest) as a driver to gather ideas in order to keep the learning current and varied is explored along with a range of pedagogical approaches used to engage children in their learning, which takes into account the notion of specific learning styles. These different approaches to learning were shared on Twitter with parents and other schools to create a wider network of shared ideas. The chapter also considers how the trial was evidenced and disseminated throughout the school, which resulted in Year 6 classrooms becoming structured to embrace a more child-led learning atmosphere. Some of the evidence collected as part of this evidence-based teaching (EBT) approach is photographs of children completing active sessions, photographs from the school's Twitter account and photographs of the learning environment.

Rationale for active learning

When meeting my new cohort, it was quickly evident that the children were passive and clearly being told what to do rather than being actively involved in and responsible for their own learning. They sat and listened in class and were able to regurgitate facts with either little or no understanding at any depth. They would solve problems in groups, but it was usually through arguments or one person taking full control (ie, doing all the work) as others sat back and watched. Children lacked independence and would constantly ask the teachers or support staff for help. They would give up at any given opportunity. It was at that point that we (my NQT and I) realised we needed to drastically change things for the children and our own mental states!

Active learning began as a 'light touch' session within lessons specifically designed to engage and excite Year 6 children in their learning. Starting a new academic year with this class (where most were working below national expectations) seemed a perfect time for me to introduce and trial active learning as a daily session. Children in the class were mostly disengaged, and although their general level of behaviour was good, their learning behaviours were poor. The children were extremely passive and struggled socially to work well in pairs or table groups. I introduced active learning to encourage the children to take responsibility for their own progress and to bring back a love of learning. I wanted something that would excite, engage and encourage children with learning, so I aligned it with the head's 'Superheroes' initiative, which was already a whole-school approach to learning. These characters were drawn from the work of Ginnis (2002) but presented as 'superhero' characters by the head to make them more appealing to children: Mr Resilient, Mr Resourcefulness, Mr Reflectiveness and Mr Reciprocal. The active sessions, although focussed around learning behaviours, needed to be used as a pedagogical approach to encourage children's deeper understating of the key concepts for reading, writing and mathematics: core subjects for improving upon Standardised Assessment Tests (SATs) taken at the end of Key Stage 2.

How the initiative was implemented

The active sessions began with my previous cohort as 'one-off' sessions in odd lessons. When children were asked to evaluate my teaching and their learning, they asked for more active learning to take place, maybe even as frequently as every session. They said they enjoyed the active session and that it helped them to remember things as they had learned for themselves rather than being told. The children were enthused about learning by doing, a type of kinaesthetic approach.

Classroom organisation helps to support active learning

I admired the way the Foundation Stage way of teaching was completely child-centred with the children taking more responsibility for their learning and being more creative with outcomes. The set-up of the Foundation Stage classroom supports this way of learning which, I feel, gets lost as the children leave the early stages of their education. A more formal set-up is required to meet the new challenges through the year groups, but I wanted to mirror the creativity and child-centred approach found at Foundation Stage in my Year 6 classroom.

We want children to be motivated and challenged by the resources that we provide for them. We want them to be thinkers, negotiators and problem solvers – to apply the knowledge that they already have to enable them to explore new possibilities.

(Bryce-Clegg, 2016)

These thoughts and ideas were timed well as along with my new class came a brand-new classroom which I was able to design (within reason!). I took the idea of zoned learning from my Foundation Stage colleagues. The shape of the tables, the availability and use of resources, and the use of displays around the classroom were all important aspects of the organisation of my classroom. I decided that I wanted the children to have round tables to promote reciprocity and discussion. There was also a horseshoe-shaped table for groups working with a facilitator/activator (teacher or teaching assistant). There was a quiet zone with clipboards to suit children who like to work away from their table. I also ordered easels for children so that they could choose to work vertically or to present work to groups or the whole class (taken from a previous piece of EBT we had conducted with the children as to their preferred writing position).

What does active learning look like?

'Active learning' is an approach to learning which engages and challenges children's thinking using real-life and imaginary games and activities. All areas of the curriculum can be enriched and developed through this pedagogical style (Ryan and Gilbert, 2011). I used active learning with my class at the start of each lesson, which was rather like using an oral and mental starter. The children were taught using a range of pedagogical strategies including self-discovery to deepen understanding. The 'active' element to the sessions included children working in pairs or groups and moving around the classroom, moving and replacing objects, taking learning outside, accessing a range of wider learning opportunities. Activities such as throwing and catching games introduced a competitive element that helped engage and excite children. The active part of the session not only bought back an enjoyment to the children's learning but also provided an emotional hook associated with a key piece of learning. This resulted in the children showing greater ability to retain information and being able to understand and apply challenging concepts across a range of subjects.

The emphasis has changed from 'teaching', through 'teaching and learning' to the situation where learning is seen as the key activity. The impact of this change should not be underestimated; it alters the fundamental premises about the status of the children, the nature of the pedagogy and the whole architecture of learning.

(Ginnis, 2002, p vii)

The idea of the active session was to 'break the mould' of the formal lesson outlined throughout the National Curriculum. Creative pedagogies were used in order to vary learning techniques and to encourage children to think for themselves.

A change of mindset to improve learning behaviours

A change of mindset was an important feature of the work as the children and I needed to learn to work together in a different way. The superheroes discussed previously were used alongside the active sessions to promote good learning behaviours. Alongside implementing active learning, I praised and rewarded good learning behaviours with visual prompts. Each activity was centred on one of the superheroes, with more focus initially on reciprocity as this was the children's weakest skill. The children would stick their name on a card which named a particular behaviour. If a child still had their card at the end of the lesson, it was a reminder to work in a particular way to ensure they lost their card. Children without cards at the end of sessions were given additional rewards (eg, a smiley face for their smiley chart). It only took a couple of weeks of training before the behaviours began to become embedded. Stickers with the superheroes were used in marking and feedback in books to re-emphasise their importance.

Learning behaviours and independence

Children had to learn to take responsibility for their own learning. They needed to see themselves as the teachers in certain situations. The superheroes helped the children identify with this approach, and the children quickly began to take ownership of their learning and to use the support of each other rather than relying on the teacher. We focussed on using the superheroes in school: Mr Resilient, Mr Resourcefulness, Mr Reflectiveness and Mr Reciprocal which resonates with Lear's assessment of how we might evidence different learning styles in the children:

> » *Independent inquirers: Young people process and evaluate information in their investigations, planning what to do and how to go about it. They take informed and well-reasoned decisions, recognising that others have different beliefs and attitudes.*

> » *Reflective learners: young people evaluate their strengths and limitations, setting themselves realistic goals with criteria for success. They monitor their own performance and progress, inviting feedback from others and making changes to further their learning.*

> » *Team workers: young people work confidently with others, adapting to different contexts and taking responsibility for their own part. They listen to and take account of different views. They form collaborative relationships, resolving issues to reach agreed outcomes.*

> » *Effective participators: young people actively engage in issues that affect them and those around them. They play a full part in the life of the school, college, workplace or wider community by taking responsible action to bring improvements for others as well as themselves.*

(Lear, 2015, pp 16–17)

When planning each active session, I took account of the four key criteria outlined above and focussed on the role of the learners (or relevant superhero) and how the children could use the superhero's particular set of characteristics as a learning approach to each activity. For example, when emphasising Mr Resourcefulness, a range of resources would be offered for each activity, some of which were better for solving the problems than others and some were not useful at all. This helped the children develop skills in assessing and evaluating which resources would be best to support their learning.

Active learning promoting the 'working classroom'

Any work created from the active session was to remain on display for the children to access whenever they needed to. Research indicates that working walls help support learning as the children can actively engage with the displays around them. However, I felt that having a literacy, numeracy and topic working wall, for example, did not support the notion of making links between the various subjects. This meant that the classroom needed to be set up as a 'working classroom' rather than just having working walls. The classroom walls were littered with work from active sessions and the children could refer to them as required during their independent work. This promoted both resourcefulness and independence, and the links formed when the children used resources interchangeably from literacy to topic for example. Eventually we began to see evidence that the children were taking a deeper approach to learning.

Consolidating and assessing learning

There were two main types of session: one where the children were required to apply their previous learning while the teacher gathered formative assessment date using an Assessment for Learning (AfL) approach and one where the children would learn something new either from the resources around them or from each other. A previous EBT project called 'Mastery' was used, where the higher-attaining children were asked to teach children working at a lower level of attainment. This would secure and deepen knowledge for the higher-attaining children and help the lower-attaining children learn from their peers. This enabled other teachers to work with selected groups to support their learning.

Lesson examples

The sessions began quite simply with games to get the attention and 'buy-in' from the children. This moved towards more complex activities where child-led learning became a focus. Some sessions would be five to ten minutes in duration, whereas others could last for a whole lesson of 40 minutes. There were lots of pictorial and concrete activities to ensure firm foundations for children's understanding linked to the Shanghai model for

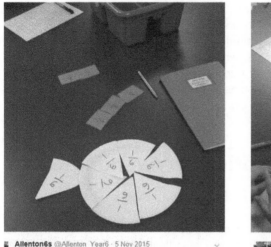

Allenton6s @Allenton_Year6 · 5 Nov 2015
For our active starter in maths we were creating a visual
representation of mixed numbers and improper fractions

Allenton6s @Allenton_Year6 · 16 Oct 2015
For our active starter in maths we were creating our own
fraction walls. Thinking carefully about fraction.

Figure 4.1 Maths activity starter

Figure 4.2 Maths activity starter using fraction walls

mastery. This is a methodical curriculum aimed at developing and embedding fluency, deep knowledge and understanding of underlying mathematical concepts. This approach to the teaching of mathematics requires the children to respond to questions and demonstrate their understanding of mathematical concepts. For example, in one particular lesson on fractions, children built and explored the fraction wall. I questioned the children's understanding and encouraged them to make links to equivalent fractions, to consider addition and subtraction of fractions, and so forth. The visual activities supported this way of learning as can be seen in Figures 4.1 and 4.2.

In some sessions the children were given a range of resources to work with. In one literacy session, the children were gathering language for a setting description of *The Chronicles of Narnia* by C S Lewis. They had a sensory box per table and the children used their five senses to explore objects from Narnia such as ice, fur, snow, pinecones, sticks, etc. The words were gathered, displayed and shared with the rest of the class. These words and phrases were then used throughout the topic to support the children's future writings on this topic (see Figure 4.3 on the next page).

As the year progressed, the active sessions were extended. For example, one lesson was used to promote British values and centred on the refugee crisis in Syria. The children were given pictures of famous refugees but were not told they were refugees. They had to work out the links between them. At this point, however, they struggled to make the links. I then shared a negative quote from the media about the refugee crisis, and this promoted some deeper thoughts and enabled the children to engage in discussions about what the media was saying regarding the ongoing crisis. I used a set of plastic balls and inserted a single

Allenton6s @Allenton_Year6 · 3 Nov 2015
Spectacular girls using their sentences to describe
the setting of Narnia

Figure 4.3 Literacy session constructing sentences following exploration of objects from sensory boxes

fact about the refugees into each one. The children then worked in groups to place these facts into positive and negative lists. The ball was then thrown to the next group. This promoted more discussion and it became clear the children were learning new facts and widening their awareness of refugees. Later on in the lesson, the children had a debate as to whether or not they would want a refugee family to move in next door. At the end of the lesson, the children looked at the famous refugee pictures again, making the links and discussing what the world would be like without these people. Because there were a few refugee children in the class, I had to be very sensitive about this issue, but this group of children wanted to share their experiences with the rest of the class. This helped everyone engage in dialogue about refugees without feeling awkward. Throughout the lesson I questioned their ideas, gave examples and assessed the children's understanding using focussed questions. When the children were asked to evaluate their learning and the lesson, they said they had done all the hard work while I and my teaching assistant did not do a lot! They said they preferred working in this way as their learning was fun, and they felt they had developed a better understanding through discovering the facts for themselves. The majority of sessions were photographed and shared on Twitter to encourage parents to engage with their children's learning, thus promoting discussions at home.

Developing and planning active sessions

As an everyday teacher dealing with the pressures and time constraints encountered by teaching staff on a daily basis, I felt that academic reading could not be a priority for me. Below is a range of sources with ideas that were gathered and developed throughout the initiative. Although there is some academic research within this chapter, it was not the sole focus of the project. In essence, I wanted something that worked, something that could be developed to suit my style of teaching. Teachers often work in isolation in the classroom where they generate great ideas to 'fix' problems. Getting teaching staff and other classroom practitioners to share these ideas in school was, however, quite a challenge.

Coming up with initial ideas was sometimes the most demanding part of the active learning sessions. I used *Teacher's Toolkit* by Paul Ginnis (2002) for pedagogical ideas alongside *Outstanding Teaching: Teaching Backwards* by Andy Griffith and Mark Burns (2014). Twitter and Pinterest were valuable forums for gathering ideas as teachers all around the world share their work. Through sharing our work on Twitter, we gathered a large group of followers from a range of educational settings from whom we were able to 'borrow' and develop ideas. My NQT and I often went out to visit other schools in her 'NQT time' in order to gather ideas and initiatives for our own teaching. This outward-facing way of working enhanced our professional development which, in turn, supported the learning back in our own classrooms.

In Table 4.1 are some additional ideas for active learning that have been adapted from original sources to suit the learners in my class. Sources were found using EBT to support research, and the ideas were trialled and developed.

Table 4.1 Ideas for active learning

Title	Role of the children	Role of the teacher
Relays: Learning to Learn (adapted from Claxton, 2003)	Questions or answers stuck around the classroom. Children to work individually, in pairs or groups to match the question and their answers	Teacher to question understanding during this session and throw in curveballs to deepen children's thinking (AFL)
Snowballs (Engaging Learners)	Thought escalation: write independently on a piece of paper, screw up and pass on. Partner to add value or challenge. Continue by questioning to deepen thinking	Teacher question to deepen thinking. Teacher could take children aside to assist their questioning using Bloom's starter stems (Bloom, 1956)

Table 4.1 *continued*

Title	Role of the children	Role of the teacher
Distillation (adapted from Ginnis, 2002)	Give children the end product. They need to 'distil' the skills by extracting them. This will find the recipe for success. This works well in maths when unpicking word problems	Teacher to gather the skills and share with the class. These skills can then be worked on and improved to promote deeper understanding of key concepts
Plastic Balls (the type you find in children's ball pits)	Empty balls of information (balls have holes in them with paper rolled up inside). Children to use this information to learn, order, match; add value for a more child-led approach. Inside or outside activity. Can be used in a circle where the balls are rolled	Teacher to fill the balls with information for the children to use. Can be true or false, facts, sentences to improve, maths problems to solve, etc during session, teacher assessing work in action
Assembly (adapted from Ginnis 2002)	Give children cards containing information. Children need to 'assemble' and match the cards. This can be at a table, outside, a relay activity, etc	Teacher using this as an opportunity for AFL while the children are working questioning for understanding
Back-to-Back (adapted from Ginnis 2002)	Pose a question or topic to the children. They sit back-to-back (one positive and one negative). Children to 'debate' the subject in turns. Could also be used as a Taboo-style game where children need to have a certain amount of time to describe the words on the cards without using that particular word. They can use synonyms and antonyms to help	The debate sessions improve speaking and listening skills. The teacher could encourage certain language features and assess. In Taboo, teacher could differentiate words according to attainment and question thinking

What was the impact?

Active learning impacted greatly on the children's learning behaviours which improved drastically. Their love of learning had clearly returned, and they wanted to work in a variety of ways. The children were able to use and apply the teachings of the learning superheroes in different situations. Lessons were fun and more varied for both the teachers and the children. As the sessions were used for both teaching and assessment, teachers were freed up to support those who really needed it to ensure a learning community where everyone received appropriate support in one way or another. It was important to keep the sessions focussed on the learning as it was easy for the 'fun element' to dominate. Every session either consolidated previous learning or introduced ideas that linked to the lesson that was about to take place. This provided greater learning links with different subject areas of the primary curriculum.

The classroom set-up enabled teachers and children to work in a variety of ways promoting both independence and team work. Children rarely asked the teachers for help, and they were openly eager to share what they had discovered. Relationships between children were strengthened, and flexible groupings enabled children to work with a wide range of peers. The mastery approach used in some sessions encouraged learners to see themselves as teachers with valid opinions to share and boosted confidence in all.

Displays encouraged children to make links between subjects and lessons. Work was rarely taken down throughout the year so that ideas from previous projects and lessons could be easily accessed. The children were encouraged to use the resources and display work around them and to leave their seats in order to do so. The use of circular tables encouraged the children to work together, particularly in skill-gathering lessons. If children began to drift off task (eg, during extended writing sessions), learning breaks with music were arranged. The learning breaks allowed the children to get up and dance, using a complete range of movements. Following the dance session, a mini plenary was used to refocus the learning. A particular favourite track of the class was Taylor Swift, *Shake It Off!*

The culture of the classroom shifted noticeably. Learning became more purposeful with children seeing the relevance in what they were doing. Lessons were fun and engaging but focussed on learning. Lessons were carefully planned to encourage learning arising directly from the children's activities. When questioned through a peer review on the school in the spring term, one girl described the learning in Year 6 as:

When you come into our classroom, you may think that Miss Poultney is lazy. She isn't often stood at the front teaching; she does all the hard work at home making sure we have all we need to learn. When in the classroom, we have to do all the hard work. She is our facilitator.

(child 1)

Academic year 2015–16 saw Allenton Primary achieve its best ever SAT results (even in a year of turmoil with new tests released by DFE (Department for Education)). It was the first year that the children scored above national average in all subject areas. The cohort entered Year 6 with only one child working at national expectations and ended with achieving 65 per cent combined in the SAT results.

Evidence gathering

Gathering appropriate evidence was tricky with active learning as the facts and figures did not tell the whole story. To evidence the culture shift, children were regularly questioned about their learning and the lessons in which they participated. They frequently judged and graded each lesson in an informal way and engaged with planning new topics with lessons and styles they preferred. Gathering the evidence in this way gave opportunities for the children to take more responsibility for their learning. Photographs and quotes from the children were also gathered as part of our evidence base.

Video evidence was gathered to share in staff meetings, which was a very effective means of disseminating our work to other teachers. These were either parts of lessons or, in some cases, whole lessons videoed using 'Class Watch', a 360-degree working video able to capture whole-class action. These videos were used in Continuing Professional Development (CPD) sessions to improve teaching and learning with teaching staff and staff external to the school on a one-to-one basis. School assessment data was used but, as we had not used a 'control group' (as in a randomised controlled trial), it was not so easy to pinpoint the measurable impact of active learning solely on the children's progress. This raises ethical issues, of course, as teachers will want to ensure that all pupils are treated equitably so that they can all benefit from the initiative. Tensions may arise between what is seen as our 'normal' professional practice and the activities that may produce sound research evidence. Val writes more about the challenges for teachers in Chapter 1. Notwithstanding these challenges, many staff noted the changes in learning behaviours of the Year 6 children, and their positive learning attitudes were noted in lesson observations and in conversations with the children. There have been changes to my approach to teaching; no longer do I feel the need to be centrestage in the classroom; this was also an approach taken by my NQT colleague. My preparation became focussed on planning resources for teaching and devising the means to engage children with various aspects of learning.

Dissemination

As part of the EBT work at Allenton, dissemination of projects such as active learning and the sharing and testing of outcomes with other teachers became essential. Active learning as a project had a huge impact on the school with changes of mindsets (for both me and the children), alterations to the classroom environment and the development of a different approach to teaching and learning. It was clear that the success of the project depended to some extent on these fundamental changes to practice which some staff found rather overwhelming. 'Selling' active learning can, therefore, be a challenge as staff may see that it requires a lot of preparatory work on their part and increased effort initially to generate ideas for different approaches to learning. As assistant headteacher leading teaching and learning, I arranged a series of staff meetings centred on discussing areas of teaching related to questioning, assessment, marking and feedback. Many of the activities within the staff meetings were delivered using the pedagogy of active learning. This enabled staff to participate with active learning while learning something new. Teachers said they enjoyed learning in this way as it gave them ideas to try in their classrooms. Later, walking around the school, I noted that some teachers were using teacher taboo, balls and snowballing in their everyday practice, sometimes without taking on the complete culture of active learning. This became a useful way of piloting the approach for teachers who felt less confident in using it and encouraging them to come into our Year 6 classrooms to observe us using this approach to learning.

Teaching- and learning-focussed culture

A teaching-and-learning display sharing ideas about different pedagogical approaches was put up outside the staffroom, and reference books linking to teaching styles were placed in the staffroom. This helped to create a teaching and learning culture that was more prominent for staff and school leaders. This drip-feed approach enabled staff to 'dip their toe' into active learning without embracing it fully as we had with Year 6. Unlike the other EBT projects described in this book, the active learning project was centred on our Year 6 groups rather than the whole school, but as the project developed, the potential for the initiative to be used in all areas of the Key Stage 2 curriculum became increasingly clear to us and other teachers.

IN A **NUTSHELL**

Active learning focuses on how children learn rather than on how teachers teach. It engages children in a series of activities designed to help them develop as active independent learners supported by their teacher rather than as passive recipients of a teacher's knowledge.

REFLECTIONS ON **CRITICAL ISSUES**

- *Sharing the outcomes of different EBT projects provides a consistent approach to children's learning.*
- *Engage teachers in your initiative by encouraging them to take on the role of learners (like the children).*
- *Disseminate the outcomes of your project more widely using social media.*

Jacqui Trowsdale and Alison Richardson

CRITICAL **ISSUES**

- *How do teachers adapt to curriculum changes by the government?*
- *Where do ideas come from for an evidence-based teaching project?*
- *How can you measure the impact of any project undertaken?*

Introduction

Prior to the university research pilot with our school, there were no overt academic partnerships which involved teachers directly. As teachers we (Alison and Jacqui) considered ourselves to be reflective practitioners, constantly assessing and developing our lessons in line with the learning needs of the children.

When presented with the idea of evidence-based teaching (EBT) by an academic (Val), the proposal seemed confusing and lacking in practical value as we already reflected on our practice on a regular basis and adapted it accordingly – so why did it need reporting and formalising? It was clear that the senior leadership team (SLT) was very interested in the idea but was struggling to pass this enthusiasm onto staff.

Reflection point

» Have you been presented with ideas that did not seem to be applicable as a practitioner? How could you act upon and interpret these ideas in a different way to improve your practice?

We discussed how we might engage with EBT based on what we had heard from Val and kept in mind the vision from the SLT, but we were less than sure what we could research from our own practice. At this time, Alison was enrolled on a Middle Leaders Programme. During the programme, several people discussed the importance of formalising reflections and asked that this was investigated within school. The SLT had also reflected upon how to disseminate the concept of EBT and initiatives within the classroom, which led them to conduct their own pilot studies that they shared in a focussed staff meeting. This staff meeting, together with the Middle Leaders Programme, caused a shift in our mindset which resulted in us being more proactive in creating our own project.

Changing curriculum and school issues: how did this affect us in the classroom?

The school is in an area of social deprivation and, not surprisingly, has a high number of pupil premium children (children receiving free school meals due to the low level of household income) on roll. The school's SAT results have been poor over many years with writing being the weakest area. Knowing this, writing was made a focus for the school. The new curriculum had just been introduced and it was apparent from reading this that the standards for literacy and especially those relating to grammar had soared. Children who had previously been just below their age-related expectation suddenly appeared less capable and so consequently had to work even harder to fill the gaps in order to catch up. In Year 3 (our year group), the push on grammar seemed particularly challenging as this had not been as explicit in the previous curriculum. Children were now required to use more technical vocabulary and have a clear understanding of what all of this meant, so we wondered how this could be made more comprehensible and accessible for the children.

Reflection points

» Consider how the new curriculum has changed schools and their foci.

» Think about the area your school is in – has this affected how/what you teach?

The identified issue and ideas to combat it

There were approximately 56 children in the Year 3 cohort. Within this year group, there was a large percentage who were achieving below age-related expectations for writing (96 per cent) based on the new curriculum. Our first approach was to put the children into two sets: a higher-attaining and a lower-attaining group to try to plug the learning gaps more efficiently and to tailor teaching specifically to their needs.

It was very clear in the higher-attaining set that, while generally the children could explain clearly what the different word types were, when it came to independent application it was equally clear that they were unsure of how to transfer this knowledge to paper. This lack of a solid foundation of understanding meant that introducing higher-level language concepts such as similes and metaphors was difficult as the children did not understand the word types well enough to be able to manipulate them.

In the lower-attaining set, it was apparent that the children struggled to identify basic word types and frequently mixed them up even in discussion, eg, describing 'and' as an adjective. This group also struggled with very basic punctuation, including the consistent application of full stops and capital letters. The children were also confused as to the grammatical structure of their sentences and rarely proofread to check that their work made sense.

At this point we had already had several informal discussions as partner teachers about the issues which were evident in the children's work; however, although we had identified what they were, we were not sure what to do about them or how complex the problem really was.

We began to consider some inquiry-type questions:

> » Were we confusing the children by offering too much variety and challenge?
>
> » To what extent should we differentiate the work of the children?
>
> » Were there differences between those children with special educational needs (SEN) (in this case, specifically dyslexia) and the rest of the cohort?
>
> » Was there any precedence for this in education and how had others dealt with it?

Through discussion we decided that the level of challenge and differentiation really could not be the root of the problem as we had used similar strategies in other subjects, and this had not affected the children's ability to perform the tasks. There was a high level of consistency within the school, and the children were used to the processes from previous years' learning. We realised that the majority of the cohort were having problems, not only those with SEN, though we did start to wonder if there was any evidence to be found in dyslexia research to further assist us.

The final point was that we just did not know if others had dealt with this before. As experienced teachers we knew that using colours generally helped children (especially those with SEN) to organise themselves better, and using different overlays/backgrounds certainly helped too. We decided to research this to confirm our opinions (or otherwise!) and discovered many research papers and websites that recommended using colour to help with organisation and memory. During this period of research, we also discovered that increasing memory recall would be key and that we could do this not only through the use of colour but also through rhyme/song.

... colour-coded – children could see each specific language feature and technique (or 'writing tool') in a different colour on the collaboratively constructed class toolkit poster. When they came to independently assessing their own or a peer's writing this helped them to establish how much of the toolkit they had used successfully.

(Rooke, 2012, p 21)

Reflection points

Consider other ways to further support children with SEN, specifically dyslexia. Refer to these websites for further support:

» www.dyslexia.com/about-dyslexia/understanding-dyslexia/ guide-for-classroom-teachers/

» www.dyslexiaaction.org.uk/for-educators

How can research for SEN be applied as good practice for all?

Final idea and implementation

Jacqui had already been using songs in an attempt to engage the children with certain word types. The songs came in the form of YouTube videos from the site www.grammaropolis.com. The children really enjoyed the characters and the catchy songs, and as teachers we felt it was really useful that the words of the songs appeared on the screen in the colour of the word type/character being portrayed. Figure 5.1 shows an example of an 'adjective character'.

We also liked that the lyrics of the songs reflected how the words should be used; the more the children listened, the more they understood and remembered the terms. This in turn gave the children a clear word bank to draw on. However, this was not enough to help the development of some children's independent application as, despite the fact that their understanding was improving, they still were not able to demonstrate this skill properly in their writing.

Figure 5.1 A picture showing the 'adjective' character from www.grammaropolis.com with words 'her' and 'ugly' in red (shown here in grey) as well as the character to reflect application of adjectives (Image courtesy of Grammaropolis LLC)

At this point we decided the children needed something more concrete to work with in order to give their writing an almost physical form. Inspired by a child from the higher-attaining set who declared 'I really like the way that when he writes an adjective it (sic) puts the noun he's describing in a colour', we decided to ask the children to start writing their actual words in colour.

We began with four colours based around what we knew to be the children's development needs and what we felt were their areas of weakness:

- » adjectives = red;
- » adverbs = green;
- » conjunctions = purple;
- » punctuation = blue.

Note that there was no song relating to punctuation, so we selected a colour that was not already connected to a song that we were using.

We practised the idea of writing a sentence while using the colour pencil crayons to write each of the words of a specific word type, eg, 'There was a large, rusty boat'. In this sentence, the 'T', ',' and '.' would be written with a blue crayon and 'large' and 'rusty' would be written with a red crayon. We realised that this method could potentially be quite difficult for the children and that it may slow them down, but we were confident that their knowledge level and ability to apply the word types and punctuation would be clearly reflected in their writing.

Every child was given a 'pack' which included the four colours. It was made clear that they would be using the pencil crayons across all curriculum subjects so that they did not feel they should apply it in Literacy only. The teaching staff also had a pack of whiteboard pens that matched the colours and each time writing was modelled by the teacher the colours would be applied. The colours were introduced in a series of lessons which also included the use of the Grammaropolis videos and songs.

Reflection point

- » Our process went from abstract via pictorial to concrete which is the reverse of what research suggests is most appropriate. Think about your own practice – what aspects of the curriculum you could make more practical/concrete to support learning?

The introduction of the colours was successful and the children were excited to make a physical connection to their understanding. Following the introductory sessions where the colours were the main focus, the process was introduced in all lessons. However, the educational topics of the subsequent lessons prevailed at all times and the colours used to support and enhance learning.

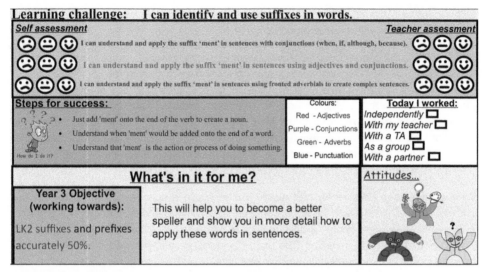

Figure 5.2 An example of learning objectives used within literacy lessons to show how colours were applied in different contexts.

Within Literacy and topic sessions the children would still cover all the aspects of the curriculum as required, but, as part of the lesson objectives, we used every opportunity available to include reference to word types and consequently the application of colours. Figure 5.2 shows some of the targets set for the children to improve their use of grammar.

The whole school was required to teach discrete grammar lessons for an hour a week (two half-hour sessions) as part of the timetabled day. After the introduction of the colours, no lessons were explicitly based around them; the grammar sessions provided an opportunity to consolidate understanding of word types and make links where necessary.

Outcomes: informal

Within the first week of the project it became very clear that the level of enthusiasm that the children had towards writing had increased. Supplying them with colour pencils and a physical way to express their understanding was a huge motivator. It did decrease the output of the children initially, but the quality of their writing was much higher and it only took them a few weeks to get back to their original pace of work.

From the teacher's perspective, it was clear from the outset that this was an immensely helpful assessment tool to gauge understanding. For example, an 'English as an additional language' child, who appeared previously to have a good understanding of the concept of conjunctions and what they are, clearly did not actually understand, as when she wrote at length she colour-coded words such as 'is' and 'the' as conjunctions and did not colour-code words such as 'and' and 'because'. This immediately impacted upon planning, leading to a lesson with a focus on conjunction.

Confusion around certain word types became much more obvious and observable. Initially, it appeared that the children were confusing adjectives and adverbs, but upon further investigation, it soon became clear that the actual misperception was around the understanding of nouns and verbs. On entry in Year 3, the children had seemed to understand these concepts quite well, but it was clear that this was an ill-founded assumption. On reflection, the fact that the children had little time working on the new curriculum meant that these word types had not been as deeply embedded or used as explicitly as we assumed they would have been.

Peer critique (see Chapter 4) had already been made a school-wide initiative, but our children (especially those in the lower set) were struggling to access it and to make helpful comments. They were finding it difficult to give examples to others as they did not have a firm understanding themselves. The use of colours really improved the effectiveness of how the children used peer critique. For example, children who generally struggled with the idea of adverbs could quickly identify whether they had been used or not by the lack of 'green' within their friend's work. While this was obviously not a foolproof system (they still struggled to confirm if some words were adverbs), it at least gave them a chance!

Reflection point

» Where possible try to bring together helpful elements of other teachers' inquiry projects so that children begin to transfer their learning across subjects and year groups. This showcases a whole-school approach to EBT.

Children's perspective on inquiry

To broaden the range of evidence for the project, we asked the children what they thought of the colours and the way they used them. Their responses were overwhelmingly positive. Below are some examples, two of which are from children whose data is featured in the next section. Note the way the children were able to use the correct terminology.

Adjectives describe a noun. The colours help me to make my work better by using more adjectives.

(child A)

I think using better conjunctions helps you add information such as using 'as well as' which is an adding conjunction. The colours remind me to use them. If I look at my work and I've missed a colour, I try to use it in my next sentence or I rub out my writing to make it better.

(child D)

It helps my work by getting me to use adjectives, adverbs, similes and metaphors.

(child E)

Outcomes: formal

As part of the project we wanted to show measurable progress. We began the programme at the start of autumn 2 (after having assessed progress at the end of autumn 1), then assessed again at the end of summer 1. To assess, we asked the children to complete an extended piece of writing which was then assessed against the Literacy curriculum objectives. Within our school we had already developed our own assessment system, moving on from 'levels'. We assessed against the objectives using the school's assessment system. The amount the children 'scored' determined their outcome – the word 'Stage' was used in place of 'Year' and the stage was divided into three parts/bands – Emerging, Expected and Exceeding. Children who were within two objectives of the next band would be given a 'plus'. The expected rate of progress between the end of autumn 1 and the end of summer 1 was two bands of progress. This was an increased rate from the year before for Year 3 as previous expectations had been to make two 'sub-levels' over the year. We were now expected to make two bands of progress over the two terms. Table 5.1 shows the progress achieved by the children.

As a cohort, Year 3 had made an average of 2.5 bands progress over the two terms – which is accelerated progress. At this point in the year the children had also closed the gap and the number of children assessed as below the age-related expectation was reduced from 96 per cent to 76 per cent. While these statistics are not as dramatic as the progress seen with bands, it still showed a closing of the learning gap between high and low achievers. While we are aware that there are other factors that could have contributed to the accelerated progress, we are confident that colour-coding played a huge part in this.

Reflection point

» When creating an EBT project it is important to assess the impact of what you have done. Consider how you will assess this – from sampling a group of children, to what evidence you will collect to demonstrate impact.

Table 5.1 Progress of Year 3 children engaging in colour-coded writing

Child	Stage at end of autumn 1	Stage at end of summer 1	Progress
Child A (LA)	Stage 0 exceeding	Stage 1 expected	+2 bands
Child B (LA)	Stage 1 expected	Stage 2 emerging+	+2.5 bands
Child C (HA)	Stage 2 expected	Stage 3 exceeding	+4 bands
Child D (HA)	Stage 3 emerging	Stage 3 exceeding	+2 bands

LA: lower achiever, HA: higher achiever.

The sample of children was selected based on the range of starting points that they presented across the year group at the end of autumn 1.

Dissemination

In conjunction with Alison's Middle Leaders Programme and the partnership with Val Poultney and the University of Derby, we were asked to produce a report outlining all aspects of colour-coding and how we applied it. We had not previously thought to share our project in school as we wanted to be sure that we had clear, measurable data gathered over a specific time frame and to avoid yet another ineffectual initiative being added to teacher workload. We began by presenting the report at the University at a conference attended by heads and deputies of local primary schools, teacher and members of the University initial teacher education (ITE) team.

After the presentation, it was clear that the school leadership team thought that colour-coding was useful and worthwhile and asked for this to be presented to the rest of the school staff with a view to whole-school implementation. This was to have a two-fold impact as, while teaching staff were interested, no other staff members other than the SLT and ourselves had carried out an EBT project. By presenting our project at the next staff meeting, we demonstrated to all the teaching staff that EBT could be a worthwhile experience for everyone, disproving the notion that this would simply be a 'tick box' exercise. Staff responded to the presentation enthusiastically and were keen to find out how they could use the scheme in their own classrooms.

Reflection point

» Sharing your EBT outcomes is a satisfying way of gathering feedback on your work, gaining confidence in what you are researching and helping to re-establish links with teachers across the school. Think about ways in which you might be able to share your work with other professionals both within and externally to your school.

School-wide evolutions

The consensus after the staff meeting was that colour-coding should be implemented across the school but amended to suit the needs of each class. The application of colour-coding across the school is shown in Table 5.2.

Personal reflections and building on our inquiry

As much as the official remit for the project was complete, we, as reflective practitioners, began the new academic year thinking about how we could improve this and adapt colour-coding for our new cohort. Looking back on our earliest lessons, it was clear that we had not always taken every opportunity to model colour-coding (even though we had every

Table 5.2 How colour-coding was implemented across year groups

Year group	Implementation and adaptation
Foundation Stage	Teachers modelled writing adjectives in red pen and collected word banks of different word types using colours
Year 1	Specific focus on punctuation (capital letters and full stop) and adjectives
Year 2	Applied colour-coding in line with Year 3 and introduced new colours for nouns and verbs
Year 4	Used strips of colour paper rather than crayons as they felt that sentence structure and ability to manipulate these word types was important
Years 5 and 6	Used colour-coding as an assessment tool whereby the children used colours to go back and underline the particular word types in their work. Other colours were introduced for prefixes and suffixes

intention of doing so) and that we had not pushed the children far enough with regard to the complexity of different word types. For example, if the children colour-coded the main adjectives within a sentence, this would have been acceptable to us at the time. However this year, we encouraged the children to think more carefully about similes, metaphors and personification and how these could be colour-coded. From this, the children evolved using red for adjectives to using red for any word or phrase that described a noun and similarly green to be used when describing verbs.

Further reflection was encountered as part of staff meetings; for instance, it was suggested that across school a new colour should be introduced for prefixes and suffixes. This brought about a healthy debate, not only within the staff meetings but within the classroom, of how word types may or may not change, eg, adding the prefix 'un' to an adjective does not change this word from being an adjective – so why use a different colour to show a prefix? Having been a cohort that opted to not do this gave our children a better understanding of how prefixes and suffixes changed the word types.

Now that colour-coding has been firmly embedded within school, we continue to reflect and develop how we teach grammar and writing, and the children now have a solid foundation to work from as they move through each year.

Thoughts on EBT

Within this chapter, we have given specific examples of how a personalised project can be developed, integrated and celebrated. Going through the process has made us appreciate how valuable evidence-based teaching is and that it is a natural extension of our good practice.

Formalising our ideas meant that we were able to measure the impact of what we were trialling. This in turn allowed us to see whether the idea worked or not which helped us to decide if it was worthwhile to keep in the classroom. Often in classrooms, it is easy to get caught in a spiral of generating and applying several new ideas simultaneously without working out if they are ideal or, indeed, beneficial. EBT allowed us to see this clearly.

We so believed in evidence-based teaching that we began another project the following year regarding handwriting. Sharing our journey within school made it more accessible for others, and hence several other teachers started their own projects in a variety of curriculum areas. Without the opportunity of the pilot and the freedom that Jon allowed his staff to have within the classroom, we both know that we would never have come up with such an innovative solution for our children.

IN A **NUTSHELL**

EBT ideas need to come organically from the staff involved and they need to be personalised to the classroom and children. With regard to teachers, they must be completed in an environment of trust and freedom to fail, and this can only come from the top, ie, the headteacher.

REFLECTIONS ON **CRITICAL ISSUES**

Recent changes in government initiatives, ie, academisation and privatisation, have led to a lack of continuing professional development (CPD) and opportunities for innovation and development for teachers and schools. During this time, the government has also chosen to 'raise the bar' in their expectations and requirements including expecting schools to develop their own assessment systems. Viewed negatively, this has been detrimental and demoralising to the teaching profession; however, it has provided the perfect platform for schools to take ownership of their own professional growth. EBT allows a forum for teachers to take control and make adaptations in a way that makes sense to them, not just the government.

It is important, in order for projects to be effective and successful, that ideas come from the teachers themselves and link directly to the children's needs. Enforcing ideas can make the projects redundant because there may be no purpose for it within a particular classroom. This also means that rather than engaging and allowing ideas, teachers feel pressured and restricted. Engagement is also an issue here and teachers who feel burdened by ideas which are not their own might feel less likely to want to be involved and follow through on the project with the correct intentions in mind.

It is integral, when any project is undertaken, to make sure its impact is measureable and clear. Without this, ideas become lost; there is a lack of clarity and a high risk that ineffective initiatives become non-negotiables within a classroom. Being able to present data gives the project a rigour it may otherwise not have.

Being involved in this project has given us a powerful sense of ownership and has made us feel more valued within our school community and allowed us to give proof of how successful we can be as teachers on a daily basis.

Jon Fordham

CRITICAL **ISSUES**

- *What is the role of leadership in establishing and embedding teacher inquiry in the school?*
- *The importance of working with an HEI academic as supporter of evidence-based teaching;*
- *Working as a role-modeller to sell change to teaching staff.*

Introduction: grassroots – setting the goals

Analogies for school leadership are two-a-penny and, more often than not, are completely abstract. As a headteacher, I could think of myself as a shepherd herding staff in the right direction, as a gardener growing staff and placing them where they will blossom and flourish, or – the one I have heard most often – I could be a bus driver who has to get the right people on the bus, the wrong people off the bus and the right people in the right seats on the bus.

But what information is out there that actually supports how to initiate and develop a learning culture in a school while improving the quality of teaching and learning outcomes for children? As a 'green-gilled' headteacher taking responsibility of a school in special measures and with a poor reputation three years ago, turning analogies into a reality was not as simple as the examples above might suggest. This was at a time when fewer teachers were entering the profession and attrition from it was greater still. So, in discussion with senior leaders of the school, and importantly with Val, the HEI academic, it became clear that research (or teacher inquiry) was one potential avenue to explore to improve the quality of teaching across the school. At the same time I could acknowledge the already large amount of discretionary effort made by the staff (the additional time that all teachers spend on their jobs above and beyond normal working hours) and provide them with dissemination outlets so that good ideas could be shared in order to raise professional awareness through a somewhat different approach to staff development. I realised that embarking on such an initiative would also give a nod towards a 'what's in it for them?' approach to continuing professional development (CPD).

The successful implementation of any new strategy in school often depends on how staff perceive the initiative. To implement evidence-based teaching (EBT) in school it was essential that staff could see the benefits of focussing their efforts on developing or engaging in research projects. Fortunately, staff were already hugely committed and passionate about the school and the learning progress of the children. The main barriers to introducing EBT and changing the mindset of staff, therefore, fell into two distinct areas.

1. Developing staff who were prepared to take risks and who would actively and overtly engage in research activities linked to school improvement priorities.

2. Formalising the EBT process to give it a strategic direction, avoiding a 'scatter-gun' approach to improvement and ensuring teacher workload remained manageable.

With Val, I also considered the overall process of introducing EBT across the school, enabling us to map out our strategy before going ahead. This strategic overview was, I felt, essential if we were all to have a good understanding of what was planned and for what reason. Essentially, EBT to be a vehicle for changing the school culture.

Reflection points

» Consider Table 6.1; it has been adapted from Davies, Davis and Ellison (nd). Working from left to right how would you respond to each of these questions?

» What areas need further support and/or resource?

Table 6.1 An example of how to introduce and implement EBT into school culture

Generate intent	Capacity building	Process to build intent	Implementation
Are senior leaders committed to promoting research? How is EBT prioritised along with other 'pressing agendas'?	Are staff 'research-ready' so capacity can be built for individuals to take on a project? What support will they require?	**Conceptualising** What will research look like in our school? **Engaging** How will staff be supported and by whom? **Articulating** How will projects be shared? Can you justify research to others? What routes for dissemination are encouraged?	Next step: Phased (individual teacher projects)/ everyone researching (whole school) and how linked with school development/ action plans? Are governors aware of these changes?

In discussion with Val, we came up with a concept for what we wanted EBT to look like in school, which was, in essence, a process for formalising what good reflective practitioners do naturally (yet often do not disseminate beyond their classrooms). We developed a simple process of plan, do, review (the action-research cycle, see Figure 3.4, page 31) but with additional rigour to support the critical evaluation of the impact of the project. We were also adamant that the project need not be onerous or large-scale.

The Allenton model

Research is often regarded by teachers as something done during their training years that bears little relevance to everyday classroom practice. I began to wonder if the term 'inquiry' or 'evidence-based teaching' could help us to bridge the challenges we face when using the word 'research'? Salles (2016, p 34) summarised this for me when he said:

It is in our teaching DNA to distrust research, because it is remote, it is ivory tower and most of all, it often doesn't correspond to our experience.

We wanted research to be rooted in the development of classroom practice, creating teachers who were critical thinkers and willing to take a risk. Projects could be of any size but always focussed on improving the quality of teaching and the level of pupil outcomes. The simple 'Plan, Do, Review' model was perfect for us, and we also kept a record of what we had researched as evidence of our work. The model is shown in Figure 6.1.

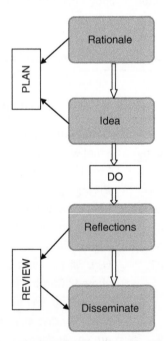

Figure 6.1 Adapting the action-research cycle to fit with 'Plan, Do, Review'

This model supported the process of critical thinking but also made the process more robust and justifiable if any visitors came to the school. It also supported staff engagement in projects, as, although research was required to plan and review the project, it was not on a scale that might put practitioners off engaging with research. We did not use control groups for example or insist on measures required for projects run by the Education Endowment Foundation (EEF) (https://educationendowmentfoundation.org.uk/) which is often the only experience teachers have of research outside their training years.

Val and I decided to kick-start research in school with an invitation to all staff to attend an afternoon workshop session with Val, who would introduce EBT and how it could be woven into daily teacher practice. The presentation, however, did not go down well. On reflection, the introduction to research for staff was far too academically oriented. The teachers needed to see the relevance of EBT to their own practice – essentially developing a 'buy-in' for the 'plan and do' stages (which teachers are naturally good at) and developing the skills necessary for the review section of the triad model over time to ensure critical and robust reflections. Ultimately, teachers needed to see practical examples of research being carried out in the school/classroom context and to be convinced of its worth before they were likely to embrace change.

The next step was to take a different approach from the workshop. With Val I created a project based on one of the school priorities (marking and feedback) as a pilot project for EBT; that could be showcased and role-modelled to the teachers. Always keen to be a visible leader, I spent time researching this topic further which happily coincided with Ofsted's use of 'Designated Improvement and Reflection Time' (DIRT). This was perfect for the project and so 'Dishing the DIRT' became a whole-school initiative. At the start of each session, and linking to Mr Reflective (one of our school learning superheroes mentioned in previous chapters), the children would spend time acting on the feedback that teachers had given. After running the project for half a term, the senior leadership team (SLT) scrutinised the children's books focussing on marking and feedback, while I spent time interviewing children and observing 'Dish the DIRT' sessions as part of the review process. In addition to these research methods, I created a staff survey in order to collect feedback on the sessions and used it as an opportunity for staff to share the successes and the downsides of the initiative.

With all the evidence gathered, Val and I sat down to look at the results. It was clear that the project was having impact with both teachers and children valuing the time allowed for making improvements to previous work and extending learning. The scrutiny of work also revealed pleasing results, and it was clear that teachers were developing children's learning through their marking. Although we were pleased that the project was making improvements to pupil outcomes, we realised that it was also a perfect vehicle for demonstrating classroom-based research and, importantly, that we could learn from our mistakes (of which I had made many!). I did not want the project to simply 'run smoothly'; how could we expect teachers to engage with EBT if I presented them with a perfect model? We wanted to show that I had made mistakes and that it was OK to take risks – for example, interviews with children, although supplying some lovely quotes about DIRT did not add any value to the critical analysis of the impact of the project, possibly due to the way in which the questions had been structured. Similarly, the staff survey which had questions with scaled score responses (Likert-type survey: 1 'agree' to 5 'disagree') did not help greatly with the analysis. However, where open responses were required (and teachers had freedom to share ideas and comments both bad and good), we could see where DIRT was having the greatest impact and how we could make improvements to further develop and refine the project. God was in the numbers, but the devil was in the details! However, both types of evidence could be used to demonstrate the impact of the project, but we realised the value of using qualitative methods as opposed to quantitative ones, and this focussed our minds on the best approaches to use in classrooms when collecting data.

Reflection points

»   Leaders often talk about being the role models in the school, but are we afraid of getting it wrong in front of staff as it may ruin our credibility?

»   How else can we encourage staff to take risks?

»   What risk would you demonstrate to your staff in your capacity as role-modeller?

In a staff meeting focussing on marking and feedback, I shared the results of the project. Obviously I was keen to make improvements to DIRT sessions, but I wanted teachers to see from the evidence gathered as part of the research that children enjoyed and valued these feedback sessions. More importantly at this stage, I wanted them to understand that the ideas they had shared on the staff survey were the most crucial of our discussion points. With this relevant information, which importantly came from them and our school context, teachers subsequently made adaptations to their sessions and used these amendments in later weeks. There was no 'hard sell' required. The second part of the staff meeting was 'the reveal' showing how this was a research project and not just another initiative. I made overt links to the start of the session where teachers were engaged because this was a project based in our school and I also shared the errors I had made and explained how collecting relevant and useful data could be a simple process. I could see that teachers were tentatively engaged; staff had seen the process work, but now it was time for them to have a go with their own ideas.

Developing EBT across the school: gaining teachers to 'buy in' to inquiry

There is a song by Rachel Plattern called *Fight Song*, in which there is a line which goes '*I might only have one match, but I can make an explosion*' (www.youtube.com/watch?v=xo1VInw-SKc).

The final part of the staff meeting was to share the Allenton model for research, or EBT as it became known to the staff. To create a culture of learning in children, we (the teachers) as leaders of learning need to show the children that we are also learners.

Reflection point

» Share with children that you are doing a project or trialling something new. Get their feedback and viewpoints on the impact of the change implemented. Role-model the learning processes you go through to children at all times.

Adopting an EBT approach in school does not mean that every teacher has to be working on a project, but, if appropriate, teachers can adapt their practice in the light of ideas from other staff. This approach meant that all staff could engage at a level with which they felt comfortable. Some decided to take on projects while others benefitted from them by adopting the practice, but the net result was the same. There was a gradual improvement in teaching, learning and pupil outcomes and we had the evidence to prove it. By sharing the leadership team's aim openly with staff, they became further engaged with projects of their own and could see that there were no hidden agendas and that everyone could benefit across the school. The next step was to give staff an opportunity to give it a go themselves.

As with any school there is a massive potential resource that lies in human resources – in this case, the school staff working within it. Excellent practice can often go unseen or is not embedded across whole school. In this sense, EBT accessed this resource and opened it up to the whole school team. This is similar to the Sky Cycle Team and their ethos of 'aggregation of marginal gains':

We said we'd take the crown off the coach's head and plonk it on the riders' heads, along with the accountability that comes with it.

(Dave Brailsford from Sky Cycle Team talking to Emma De Vita,
Management Today, 2010 (2013))

This was an example of an approach which came as a shock to some of the young Team Sky riders.*'But it's very empowering'*, says Brailsford, admitting that sometimes he has been amazed at how strict the riders are with themselves, a bit like teachers. He likes to think of himself as an orchestral conductor.

'I believe that a group of people have far greater expertise in their individual fields than I will ever have, so there's very little point asking them to pass me their instrument when they play it wrong so that I can have a go – though it's a massive instinct to do that', he laughs. 'But that would be a huge mistake'.

(De Vita, ibid)

As with the conductor, as headteacher I am reminded that each teacher has far greater classroom expertise (teacher agency), and as with gestalt, the sum of their collective agencies is greater than the sum of their parts. EBT at Allenton embodied this ethos, but the accountability needed to be carefully approached, as allowing teachers the freedom to take risks was essential if the project was to be successful.

To build the momentum, I shared the peer critique initiative with all the staff (see Chapter 3) and explained that it was going to be a project run by senior leaders (alongside other projects) and made it clear that they could all engage if they chose to do so. I shared prompts as starting points, linking these to the school priorities for other projects that staff may be keen to develop. This was followed by a staff meeting a few weeks later led by members of the SLT where the projects they had been working on were discussed and peer critique, teaching superheroes to support Year 1 transition and mastery projects were all shared with staff. It was important to ensure that staff were fully aware of these projects and what an EBT project might entail, but information given during the staff meetings also afforded opportunities for me to keep the projects prioritised within the meeting agenda. There was a shift from me as a headteacher driving projects to 'trusting' teachers as professionals to drive teaching and learning in their classrooms and in wider contexts.

A fortunate unplanned occurrence during these early stages of EBT development and implementation at school helped to give further credence to this work. During this time we had a final-year BEd student trainee from the local university in a member of the SLT's classroom, so she was able to witness the class teacher's efforts with her research. This motivated her to engage with some of the projects in school and helped her to develop her classroom practice bringing together the theory of research from lectures at the university with practical research conducted in the primary classroom. Having an experienced member of SLT presenting her own EBT project alongside a student teacher really reinforced to me (and others) that research should be an activity carried out by all teaching professionals at whatever stage of their career. I know that later in the year the BEd student wrote an excellent dissertation on her research project which she and her mentor presented to incoming final-year students at the university in order to engage them more fully in their final-year project. Ultimately she was employed in the school as a Year 6 teacher.

Reflection point

» Bringing together the theory and practice of EBT is a vital role for universities engaged in teacher education. This was an excellent example of how a student trainee's own understanding of how research can take place in the primary classroom with benefits for her own dissertation's outcomes. How can your initial teacher education (ITE) partnership with schools work to encourage EBT approaches in school under challenging circumstances? How can your trainees help schools with this?

Over the next term and a half, EBT gained momentum. Projects began to appear and staff spoke openly about ideas they were trialling. It was rather like dropping a pebble in a pond with good ideas being shared and good practice spreading like ripples across the school. Some projects developed into whole-school projects such as peer critique and colour-coded writing, while others were restricted to specific year groups as they were bespoke approaches for that cohort or year group's needs. There was a clear shift in culture at the school. It can feel like a lonely place in some schools when a sole person (usually the headteacher) is the driver for teaching and learning, but the development of a more collegiate approach where anyone can take responsibility for leading a project and improving outcomes in school beyond their own classroom was very much welcomed by me.

Reflection point

» Look at the graph in Figure 6.2. Using the four letters shown in the key (A, P, Q and R) and thinking about your context, plot them for how much time is spent by teachers on each area.

From experience, most teachers would plot the letters as shown in Figure 6.3. Teachers focus, rightly, on teaching and progress. Teachers can perceive that research is not something they do and that it has little impact on learning in the classroom. Similarly, focussing children's attitudes to learning is something that teachers do instinctively (if not overtly) and so is seen to have greater importance despite the fact that it may not impact on outcomes.

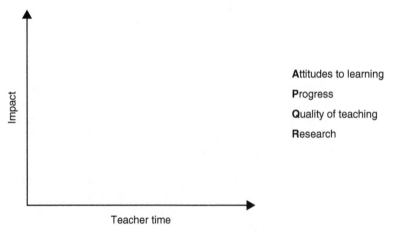

Figure 6.2 Measuring the impact of different teacher activities as related to time spent on them

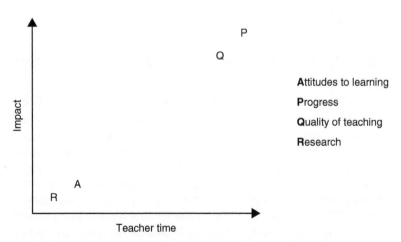

Figure 6.3 Example of how teachers might plot A, P, Q and R

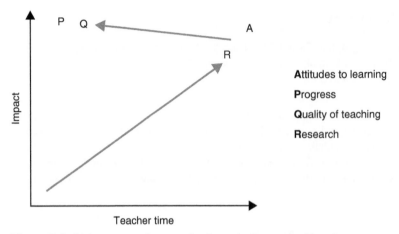

Figure 6.4 Giving research a greater focus in the work of teachers

At Allenton we saw a shift as seen in Figure 6.4. The research initiative centring on the promotion of children's skills and attitudes to learning resulted in a greater focus on the quality of children's learning and less time on the quality of teaching (to find out more about attitudes to learning, read back Chapter 4 or look at Paul Ginnis' (2002) book entitled *Teacher's Toolkit*, or Jonathan Lear's (2015) *Guerrilla Teaching*).

Evidence-based teaching supports critical reflection of practice. If something is not working, then teachers need the time and space to think and discuss their research ideas with peers (see Chapter 2). Time is also required to put these systematically into practice by following the 'Plan, Do, Review' model to ensure impact.

Embedding and maintaining the culture change

You're going to make a difference. A lot of times it won't be huge, it won't be visible even. But it will matter just the same.

Commissioner Gordon from *Batman* (Brubaker and Ruka, 2004)

Many educators enter the teaching profession to make a difference, and much of that goes unseen. Somewhat ironically, teachers can become introverted and class-focussed due to this vocational 'calling'. While EBT maintains the focus on outcomes for children, engaging with the process has helped teachers to look beyond their classrooms (above and beyond what they naturally do) to find ideas to engage their pupils and to consider the impact of their work across the school. This mind shift was a far easier task than getting teachers on board with EBT. Val was always keen to promote the projects that teachers had taken on and insisted that the teachers themselves should do the 'telling'. We set up regular opportunities for staff to disseminate their practice in staff meetings and through network meetings with the Derby Teaching Schools Alliance (DTSA). We also created an in-school project display outside the staffroom so that there was a visual presence of EBT with resource packs and thus staff could apply the ideas in their classes. Through these initial stages where we shared ideas at different forums, more schools became interested in EBT and visited our school to see current projects in action or to discuss EBT approaches more generally.

Teachers were initially tentative about such visits and were clearly uncomfortable with the notion of sharing ideas out of school, but taking this step was the most important one of all. It created pride in our school. When I began working at Allenton, teachers often shared how they would hide or mumble to others that they worked at the school, but as the project developed they were eager to share where they worked because the external perception of our school was beginning to change. This immeasurable 'feel good factor' acted like a positive feedback loop driving teachers forward. Val and I wanted to maintain the momentum and continued to explore other routes so that the projects could be shared. This initially entailed either one or both of us sharing EBT practice with larger groups such as the Teacher Education Advancement Network (TEAN), Challenge Partner hubs, universities and other teaching schools. Once the interest was sparked, it was the teachers or senior leaders of Allenton who would visit other schools to promote EBT to share ideas. Over the year, Val and I had regular meetings and shared numerous emails. Neither of us appreciated the journey the school had taken in such a short space of time in achieving positive outcomes for the children and professional development opportunities for the staff. Val wanted to put on a celebration event at the university in order to provide another opportunity for teachers to present their projects and for the school to celebrate the work over the year. Val booked the university venue for a full day and invited headteachers, teachers, students and teaching school leaders to attend the morning session. Jacqui and Alison have reported their experience of this event in Chapter 5.

The afternoon session at the university was just for Allenton staff only, and this allowed us the space to reflect on the past academic year. Like many schools, we have non-negotiables or evidence of success documents, and I was eager to use this opportunity to tie together the threads of the different projects that had been going on in the school. I had clarity in my mind which projects needed to be whole-school from the data analysis, but I wanted to maintain the collegial approach with staff. So with the school priorities for the next academic year shared, we, as a staff group, went through the projects methodically and weaved them into our teaching and learning document, outlining what each of the projects would look like in class. This was far easier said than done, it often felt like herding cats, but it was an important process to go through as it gave EBT a strategic direction and ensured good practice 'whole-school' for any late adopters. It also gave us an opportunity to review the document as some projects superseded certain practices or became surplus to requirements. It was important that teachers could see that we were not asking them to do more and that we were managing their workload.

Reflection point

» Although not a believer initially (I was focussed on the impact in school), giving staff the chance to share the outcomes of their work proved invaluable for maintaining and embedding EBT in school. What opportunities could you provide for staff to share and disseminate research practice both in and out of school?

External links can be more difficult to arrange, but Teaching School Alliances (TSAs) are a good place to start as they are required to have a research section as part of the 'Big 6' ideas. Challenge Partner and mathematics hubs are valuable outlets, and members are always keen to share ideas. Twitter is a fabulous place to share ideas (Helen does this in Chapter 4; see photographs of her Twitter feed on pages 40–1) and to find new ones, but I always have in mind 'Never has so much been written to be read by so few' when using Twitter. So think carefully about how you build up and present your profile.

The future and where do we go now as a school?

Anyone can be cool, but awesome takes practice.

(Lorraine Peterson, 1998)

For me, the culture of a school is all in the background – beyond the voices and bustle of everyday school life. It is the buzz and the hum of a machine as the cogs work. For something to change the culture of an institution ('the way we do things around here'), it needs to be powerful enough to become a habit – something that you begin to do instinctively. Using EBT as an initiative to move the culture forward so we could embrace it as part of our normal everyday practice meant that I had to take a leadership role and lead from the front while subsequently keeping a hand on the tiller, steering from behind. The baton for EBT needed to be passed on to other senior leaders in school so that I was less central to the change process. It would also give others a chance to head up projects and take responsibility for EBT across the school. As a result we created two roles: an EBT 'Horizon Scanner' and an EBT 'Advocate'. The idea of the Horizon Scanner role was someone who would gather recent research, find ideas and share these with staff. The Advocate would put these ideas into practice and disseminate results. (In practice we found that these roles were often blurred.)

Both senior staff who took on these roles maintained the systems put in place over the year and became sounding boards for ideas and problems staff might be experiencing in class. They also rolled the EBT project out to support staff, getting teaching assistants and mentors involved in research projects and reflecting on their own practice. In this way EBT became embedded in the school, and teachers naturally took risks and trialled ideas as they came across them. Our journey took teachers who were reluctant to engage in research to a point where some became fervent advocates for teacher inquiry. For others it certainly supported and enhanced their level of critical reflective practice. The outcomes for the school continue to improve (as evidenced by our very agreeable SAT results in 2016), and as teachers move to various schools and new teachers enter Allenton, we encourage them to engage with an EBT project. The main difficulty with maintaining the momentum is that, at present, not many other schools practise in the same way. Some staff have said, *'When do we get something back? We share our good ideas all the time but very rarely do other schools!'* With this in mind we set up a Teacher Think Tank to encourage interested practitioners to discuss and share research and practice. Although still in its early days, I believe the Think Tank has potential as does the increase in 'Teachmeets' across the country, which are great places for sharing ideas.

Reflection points

Nationally, school-based research is going from strength to strength, and there is a wealth of information about EBT and action research. There is also a drive to engage teachers in research, but like the staff at my school, do we put them off it at the outset?

» Is it accessible to busy teachers?

» What can we change to encourage teachers to engage in their own research?

» How might this impact on school culture?

IN A **NUTSHELL**

There is almost an inexhaustible supply of books which inform teachers on how to become the ideal or perfect teacher. As school leaders however, do we actively create a culture that supports this or, like the books, do we tell them how it is done? Teacher inquiry or EBT has been crucial in creating a culture in Allenton School where self-improvement and critical self-reflection are fostered. By developing a teacher-led model for continual professional development (through a culture of EBT), initiatives can be implemented quickly, and the generation of new ideas can come directly from the teacher's head rather than the head's desk, resulting – I believe – in much greater impact in the classroom.

REFLECTIONS ON **CRITICAL ISSUES**

This chapter has mapped out the journey of our school and is written as a story of the main stages and events we went through as a whole-staff group. What is not mapped out is the crucial nature of the professional dialogue I had all the way through with other colleagues, headteachers, TSA leads and classroom teachers. The support and input given by Val throughout the pilot year was important for me. Her deep roots in academic research gave 'teeth' to the projects and, through her constant encouragement, enabled me to translate this into practice.

Val Poultney

CRITICAL **ISSUES**

- *What are the most important issues in introducing, embedding and sustaining an evidence-based teaching approach to school improvement?*
- *What are the key learning points for school leaders and teachers?*
- *How do you assess whether your school is research-interested or research-engaged?*

Introduction

None of us working at Allenton Primary could have predicted how well the implementation of evidence-based teaching (EBT) was to go across the school or the impact it would have on school leaders, teachers and children. Val's academic guidance along with Jon's experience and expertise helped us to plan the initial introduction of EBT in school, but it is fair to say that future steps were based on our reflections of 'what worked' and how we could continue to engage staff with the initiative in the future. Reflecting on our work over the past two years, we may well ask ourselves how we might do things differently the next time around. Of course, this is a challenge to answer: that there will always be different schools, different contexts and different approaches to EBT might be our first response. We have found no definitive EBT model – no 'recipe' approach for how primary schools can begin to engage with and sustain an EBT approach over time so that it is successful. That said, we have identified some generic issues which we think are worthy of some further discussion, and they are presented in this concluding chapter. We begin with the school leaders and the teachers, go on to discuss some further thoughts about school–university partnerships and finally consider a matrix approach identifying EBT characteristics that practitioners can use to establish how engaged a school is with EBT.

Practitioners: what did they learn?

In their accounts of how they engaged with EBT, teachers and school leaders raised many learning points that were both beneficial and challenging. EBT became a route through which tacit teacher knowledge could be made explicit, could change teacher practice and make an impact on learning that could be shared with other professionals. To become a researching teacher seemed at first a daunting prospect, but fears were allayed through the role-modelling exercise carried out by Jon and the senior leadership's engagement with Val's pilot research. This served to showcase EBT as a possible solution to some of the everyday teaching problems that were being reported and evidenced at Allenton Primary. Coupled with the new SAT in 2015 and the government drive for a 'deep thinking' curriculum, some teachers saw EBT as an opportunity to rethink their practice.

Over the past two years, we have seen EBT projects which have made teachers think more deeply about their practice. Table 7.1 summarises some of the key points of leadership and teacher learning which are given in more detail in Chapters 3–5.

Table 7.1 What teachers learnt from engaging with an EBT approach

Learning point	What has been learnt by practitioners?
Knowledge assimilation	• How to make tacit knowledge explicit and relevant to practice • Ownership of teacher knowledge in specific context • Using teacher-generated knowledge to make informed decisions about children's learning
Focus on learning	• Child-centred learning central to classroom practice • Teacher as facilitator/activator of learning • Redesigning the classroom to find new learning spaces eg, working walls • Improved behaviour as linked to new and creative ways of learning • Children's social interaction is improved, eg, through peer critique • Establishing an emotional bond with learning through active learning, children become more independent learners
Formalising teacher reflections	• Rooted in raising standards, so a good place to begin problematising learning • Linked to learning and using inquiry (research) questions to help give focus to EBT project • Providing a more analytical and evaluative lens for reflection, leading to critical self-reflection

Table 7.1 (*continued*)

Learning point	What has been learnt by practitioners?
Ownership	• Ideas for EBT must come from teachers' own practice and be owned by them • Powerful force for having control over one's own professional development: re-professionalises teachers • Impact is vital and should be measurable (but this can be a challenge to evidence immediately and may occur over time) • EBT as an extension of what is seen to be good professional practice as possibly related to the early training of teachers
Dissemination	• Sharing/adapting outcomes of other teachers' EBT projects for use in your own classroom • Encouraging practitioners from other schools to review/ share your work (although sharing can be a one-way endeavour!) • Use staff meeting agenda to include updates and progress of EBT projects across the school • Disseminating EBT outcomes to parents and wider audiences via social media • Headteacher dissemination to encourage building of external networks and credentials for EBT • Engaging with professional and academic events to further promote EBT
Social issues	• Changes to practice and learning may cause a shift in approaches to school learning culture which are more positive than before • Teachers feel trusted to do their work as professionals (linked to ownership of EBT) • They gain more confidence and are willing to share their work within school and externally (see Dissemination) • They become more collegial, form networks (within and external to school) • They build capacity and agency for change generally (teachers engage more with what is going on across the school)

(continued overleaf)

Table 7.1 (*continued*)

Learning point	What has been learnt by practitioners?
Research issues	• What is the difference between good professional practice and ethical research in the classroom? • Adapt ethical issues to reflect the professional landscape – a role for the HEI academic perhaps? • Research methodologies have to be adapted to fit the classroom context. Action research is a good starting point • Evidence can be collected over a range of formats, not just statistical data. Videos of lessons, photographs and anecdotal stories are all evidence • Teachers must decide what constitutes good evidence for showcasing impact • Decide on your moral boundaries: no use of control groups perhaps?
Leadership	• Teachers become leaders of learning in their own classrooms • Teachers gain confidence and challenge school leadership, not always productively • Be open to sharing leadership as colleagues gain confidence and influence other teachers • Adoption of new roles to sustain EBT over time (EBT advocate, for example) • Reflections on next steps with EBT and working with academic • Head as architect, structural reformer to facilitate EBT across school • Establishing professional dialogues with teachers • Realising and releasing hidden staff potential • What role for governance beyond receiving information about the project?
Issues for the university	• How to embed EBT approaches into the initial teacher education (ITE) curriculum? • Ways in which trainees gain knowledge about EBT and have experience of it in placement schools • Ways in which positive outcomes of EBT can be used to assist school improvement more widely • What research helps us to better evaluate the worth of EBT in primary schools? • How to ensure teachers become more ethically research-aware

Dissemination of practitioner research

One of the most powerful ways of engaging teachers in their own professional development is through discussion and dissemination of EBT. Jon was already an advocate of this approach. He was comfortable with presenting to external audiences and already had a presence externally through the school through heads' meetings. Jon put EBT as a priority item on the staff meeting agenda and disseminated his (initially failed) attempt to research the DIRT (Dedicated Improvement Reflection Time) project to all the staff. Following this meeting, other teachers were encouraged to present their work, so this agenda item became the 'safe space' for teachers to share their experiences with EBT. While presenting to ones' peers might have been a normal practice for Val and Jon, it was certainly not routine practice for teachers at Allenton Primary. The opportunities for teachers to share practice were very limited prior to the beginning of our work, yet soon after that first staff meeting, we found evidence of teachers informally discussing and sharing their practice within classrooms, corridors and the staffroom.

Over time, these informal discussions became internal networks across the school between Foundation Stage, Key Stages 1 and 2. These networks helped teachers support each other in the development of their respective inquiries, a form of 'joint practice development' (JPD) (Sebba, Kent and Tregenza, 2012). Some teachers like Helen (see Chapter 4) had begun to use social media such as Twitter and Pinterest to disseminate the work and engage with professional audiences and parents more widely. Symbolically, too, the evidence for embedding EBT was also being seen in the various display boards within classrooms and in the corridors. The senior team had designated a display board outside the staffroom containing information about EBT, recent articles, relevant courses related to researching teachers, the Teacher Education Advancement Network (TEAN) conference, photographs and so forth. As Jon and the senior team began to see the value of EBT, they too disseminated the work more widely in their respective meetings external to the school. This resulted in staff from other schools in Derby and Derbyshire making visits to Allenton to see the progress of the work. From an academic perspective, Val was developing research and development through the Derby Teaching Schools Alliance (DTSA) and presenting the work in the relevant academic context. Ultimately, the dissemination routes merged together and, on behalf of Allenton Primary, Jon and Val presented the progress of the EBT work at the TEAN conference in May 2015 and oversaw the publication of a paper (based on the research Val did with the senior leadership team: see Chapter 2) and finally managed the publication of this book.

Learning points

1. Dissemination in its many forms is the best way to keep a project alive: everyone can have a voice in it or write about it or evidence it in their professional practice.

2. Allow everyone to play to their strengths: professionally, heads and teachers understand how to disseminate the work within and external to school; academics can advise on conferences, papers and books.

School–university partnerships: what have we learnt?

School–university partnerships are the mainstay of teacher education programmes where university trainees carry out their school placements. The partnership between Val and Jon was a different arrangement; both of us had leadership experience (Val first in school and latterly in the university; Jon previously as deputy head and now as headteacher). Not surprisingly, both of us approached this work from different viewpoints, contexts and cultures. However, our collective goal was the same; we both saw EBT as a solid approach to school improvement that went beyond one-off fashionable initiatives. We wanted to use an approach that would not only raise standards but that would also provide the means for teachers to engage with professional development and provide opportunities for them to reflect on their practice in a safe, non-judgmental space. As an experienced teacher, Val was very aware of the need to tread carefully, particularly during the early stages of the work, and did not want to encroach on teachers' professional territories. Southworth (2000, p 20) summarises this as:

'working with' colleagues, rather than 'working on' practitioners, is more productive and ultimately more powerful because the sharing of ideas is so stimulating and challenging.

The foundation of this partnership rested upon establishing and developing a growing working relationship with the head, senior leadership team (SLT) and practitioners who engaged with EBT. Headteachers and academics come from very different cultures; for schools, the pace of work is much faster and is focussed on impact and improvement, whereas for academics, the pace appears to be much slower, with time for thinking and reflection. Sometimes, convincing heads of the worth of inquiry is not always straight-forward, and although few would dispute the benefits of teacher inquiry, headteachers may be less inclined to provide the architecture and resources to develop it over time. In order for inquiry to be properly established, factors such as these have to be understood and considered alongside other leadership roles related to performance management and target setting. There are many competing priorities for school leaders to consider, and academics have to be aware of these pressures as part of their role as 'supporters', 'dialogic critical friends' or 'knowledgeable others'. The role for an academic as another leader of learning is a compelling one (Ebbut, Worrall and Robson, 2000; Moss, 2008; Nelson and O'Beirne, 2014), but how does this relationship work in practice? It can be helpful to try to work out the nature of this relationship considering such issues as:

» agreeing the reasons why EBT is being introduced (eg, as a means of school improvement or shift in school culture);

» recognising each other's experience and strengths when sharing out tasks;

» focus and scope of the research being undertaken;

» how and when to communicate with each other.

We developed a form of reciprocal leadership where ownership of the work was shared, a benchmark for change was established, and a starting point for the work agreed. Working as equals, we endeavoured to build collective responsibility for learning throughout the school, adopting a flexible approach so we could maintain (over time) a dynamic partnership. As Val spent more time in school than Jon did in the university, she began to move from a position of outsider to insider. This idea of insider-outsider where the hyphen becomes the shared space is where shared beliefs, understandings and a common language can be developed (Broadhead, 2010; Drake and Heath, 2011). Not only was Val inhabiting a space with Jon, but also with the teachers, as inquiry practices were developed.

Learning points

1. Productive partnerships are built on trust, take time to develop and are based on shared goals.

2. Academics need to understand school culture and adapt their work to that context.

3. Leadership from the headteacher and SLT are vital to introducing, embedding and establishing an EBT route over time.

How do you know if your school is moving towards an inquiry culture?

Looking back over the last two years, it is possible to see the evolution of EBT and how it was possible to change the culture of the school where at least some of the teachers were engaged in their own classroom inquiry (research). One of the challenges for school leadership and competing school priorities is keeping EBT high on the agenda. As already explained, Jon created EBT Advocate and Horizon Scanner roles to privilege the work and to keep it current. Thinking about the pace of the work, we came up with the 6Es model (see Table 7.2) that lists the characteristics of each stage of EBT evolution. We think this might help school leaders especially in deciding where they are in the implementation of EBT and give some guidance as to their next steps. We also suggest that it is a useful working document that can be used to evidence a school journey from one that is research-interested to one that is research-engaged.

Table 7.2 Creating a professional/academic learning community: a maturity matrix for moving towards an inquiry culture

1. Establishing	2. Emerging	3. Evolving	4. Embedding	5. Excelling	6. Evangelising
Failings as identified, eg, by the inspectorate, may be a driving force for future change. Whole-school improvement is led by headteacher or members of the SLT normally using bought-in packages from external providers or ideas from other schools.	Strategically there is preparation for introduction of EBT through development and action plans. All staff are included in this vision, as well as the governing body. There is a time frame in place for the start and length of time for the EBT project to run. Resource implications such as staff cover, teaching resources and additional meetings have been considered.	Identify the staff who have the confidence to trial new ideas they have discovered to improve their own practice. Consider how these new ideas are evaluated and how they may be shared beyond the individual's classroom. School leadership is linking the action points agreed on the development plan to evidence impact of projects and move towards disseminating outcomes to the wider school staff.	Senior leaders engage and role-model the use of EBT to demonstrate practice to other members of staff. Senior staff provide opportunities for teachers to share their EBT work with other staff and to engage in critical reflection. Consider what evidence best illustrates impact of EBT approaches. School data is readily available and HEI academic can advise further.	EBT is a strategic part of school improvement. All staff are engaged in and supported to develop EBT in order to raise outcomes for pupils. Staff members 'horizon scan' for new ideas and have a network of partnerships to draw and share new ideas. Experienced staff support the baselining of projects, and evaluations are rigorous in order to determine the impact of EBT cycles.	EBT is embedded practice and an integral part of the school ethos and culture. There is a passion for researching practice evident in school and in the wider locality. There is a relentless drive by leaders to maintain and improve a culture of leading teaching using evidence-based routes Staff actively seek out and support external partnerships with other schools, trusts, alliances.

Table 7.2 (continued)

1. Establishing	2. Emerging	3. Evolving	4. Embedding	5. Excelling	6. Evangelising
Outstanding/ good staff routinely trial new ideas they have discovered … no formalisation of the impact or outcomes of these endeavours. Impact measures are not well understood or documented.	An academic adviser has been sourced. There may be some links to HEI by individuals usually if some staff are undertaking higher level qualifications. The headteacher is taking a lead on the project and is passionate about EBT as a school improvement vehicle.	Evidence of EBT is beginning to appear around the school and not confined to individual classrooms.	Dissemination work is building, but partnerships with other schools are limited.	Peer reflection and analysis is used effectively to determine future projects and inform planning of teacher CPD. Staff disseminate their projects across the school and these form an integral part of the school improvement cycle.	Fully planned engagement with HEI academic routes often linked to ITE. Teachers engage with university ITE trainees in school and at the academy, through lectures, seminars and in the school classroom to promote EBT.

IN A **NUTSHELL**

The success of EBT as a vehicle for improving teaching, learning and development of practitioners is dependent on effective and supportive school leadership; we suggest between the headteacher, SLT and a university colleague who can work as a critical friend with school colleagues providing support as necessary. Keeping EBT integral to the school action plans and charting its progress gives everyone the opportunity to evaluate the outcomes of the evidence collected through appropriate dissemination channels.

REFLECTIONS ON **CRITICAL ISSUES**

The next steps for the staff of Allenton Primary involve taking the school from an ungraded Ofsted outcome to one that is at least 'Good' or beyond. The school is now an academy and part of a Nottingham Trust. The results of the 2016 SAT tests have been very encouraging, and the school is currently ranking third out of nine trust schools. Jon hopes that what his staff see as educationally desirable also counts as educationally effective when the inspectorate visit early 2017. Their job at Allenton is to break the tradition that children from deprived wards of Derby are always going to underperform and to change the teaching and learning mindsets of staff and children to a more positive outlook. We are all convinced of the merits of EBT as an all-round school improvement initiative. This book is testimony to our vision.

REFERENCES

Ainscow, M, Dyson, A, Goldrick, S and West, M (2016) Using Collaborative Inquiry to Foster Equity Within School Systems: Opportunities and Barriers. [online] Available at: www.tandfonline.com/doi/full/10.1080/09243453.2014.939591 (accessed 24 January 2017).

Beckett, L (2016) *Teachers and Academic Partners in Urban Schools: Threats to Professional Practice.* London and New York: Routledge.

Berger, R (2003) *An Ethic of Excellence.* Portsmouth, NH: Heinemann.

Bhabha, H K (1994) *The Location of Culture.* New York: Routledge.

Biesta, G (2007) Why "What Works" Won't Work: Evidence-Based Practice and the Democratic Deficit in Educational Research. *Educational Theory,* 57(1): 1–22.

Bloom, B S, Engelhart, M D, Furst, E J, Hill, W H and Krathwohl, D R (1956) *Taxonomy of Educational Objectives: The Classification of Educational Goals. Handbook I: Cognitive Domain.* New York: David McKay.

Broadhead, P (2010) 'Insiders' and 'Outsiders' Researching Together to Create New Understandings and to Shape Policy and Practice: Is It All Possible? in Campbell, A and Groundwater-Smith, S (eds) *Connecting Inquiry and Professional Learning in Education: International Perspectives and Practical Solutions.* London and New York: Routledge.

Brubaker, E and Ruka, G (2004) *In the Line of Duty.* DC Comics.

Bryce-Clegg, A (2016) How ABC Does. [online] Available at: www.abcdoes.com/abc-does-a-blog/2016/01/common-play-behaviours-and-continuous-provision/ (accessed 22 January 2017).

Carter, A (2015) Carter Review of Initial Teacher Training (ITT). [online] Available at: www.gov.uk/government/uploads/system/uploads/attachment_data/file/399957/Carter_Review.pdf (accessed 24 January 2017).

Claxton, G (2003) Learning to Learn: A Key Goal in a 21st Century Curriculum. [online] Available at: http://escalate.ac.uk/downloads/2990.pdf (accessed 15 January 2017).

Coleman, A (2007) Leaders as Researchers: Supporting Practitioner Enquiry Through the NCSL Research Associate Programme. *Educational Management Administration and Leadership,* 35(4): 479–97.

Davies, B, Davies, B and Ellison, L (nd) Success and Sustainability: Developing the Strategically-Focused School. National College of School Leadership. [online] Available at: www.brentdavies.co.uk/Web%20Articles/NCSL%20~%20Strategy.pdf (accessed 10 January 2017).

Davis Dyslexia Association International (1995–2016). [online] Available at: www.dyslexia.com/about-dyslexia/understanding-dyslexia/guide-for-classroom-teachers/ (accessed 11 January 2017).

Department for Education (2013, updated 2014) National Curriculum. [online] Available at: www.gov.uk/government/collections/national-curriculum (accessed 24 January, 2017).

Derby Teaching School Alliance Strategic Advisory Group (2016). [online] Available at: http://dtsa.org.uk/about/strategic-advisory-boards/dtsa-primary-cpd-leadership-research-strategic-advisory-group/ (accessed 23 January 2017).

De Vita, E (2010 [2013]) Sky Take on the Tour de France. [online] Available at: www.managementtoday.co.uk/dave-brailsford-sky-tour-de-france/article/992254 (accessed 21 January 2017).

DfES (2001) *National Literacy Strategy: Improving Writing.* DfES Publications.

Dolmans, D, Wolfhagen, I and Ginns, P (2010) Measuring Approaches to Learning in a Problem Based Learning Context. *International Journal of Medical Education,* 1(1): 55–60.

Drake, P and Heath, L (2011) *Practitioner Research at Doctoral Level: Developing Coherent Research Methodologies*. London and New York: Routledge.

Dyslexia Institute Limited (2005–15). [online] Available at: www.dyslexiaaction.org.uk/for-educators (accessed 22 January 2017).

Ebbut, D, Worrall, N and Robson, R (2000) Educational Research Partnership: Differences and Tensions at the Interface between the Professional Culture of Practitioners in Schools and Researchers in Higher Education. *Teacher Development*, 4(3): 319–36.

EL Education (2012) Austin's Butterfly. [online] Available at: www.youtube.com/watch?v=hqh1MRWZjms (accessed 20 January 2017).

Fordham, J and Poultney, V (2015) Whoa, This Is Massive, This Is Huge: Leading the Inquiry-Focused Primary School: A Critical Examination of Senior Leaders' Experiences of Introducing and Leading Inquiry from an East Midlands Primary School under Special Measures. Conference paper presented at the Teacher Education Advancement Network (TEAN), May 2015. [online] Available at: my.cumbria.ac.uk/Public/Education/.../2015/ValPoultneyAndJonFordham.pptx (accessed 7 March 2017).

Fordham, J, Poultney, H, Poultney, V and White, J (2015) Derby Teaching School Alliance Heads Conference, 2015. [online] Available at: http://dtsa.org.uk/conferences/dtsa-annual-school-leaders-residential-conference/ (accessed 21 January 2017).

Foreman-Peck, L and Murray, J (2009) Action Research and Policy, in Bridges, D, Smeyers, P and Smith, R (eds) *Evidence-Based Education Policy: What Evidence? What Basis? Whose Policy?* Chichester: Wiley-Blackwell.

Ginnis, P (2002) *Teacher's Toolkit: Raise Classroom Achievement with Strategies for Every Learner*. Carmarthen: Crown House.

Goldacre, B (2013) *Building Evidence into Education*. Department for Education. [online] Available at: www.gov.uk/government/uploads/system/uploads/attachment_data/file/193913/Building_evidence_into_education.pdf (accessed 22 January 2017).

Grammaropolis (2009–16). [online] Available at: www.grammaropolis.com (accessed 27 January 2017).

Grammaropolis (2012) Paint the Way. [online] Available at: www.youtube.com/watch?v=5hIqdPrH-k (accessed 24 January 2017).

Greany, T (2015) How Can Evidence Inform Teaching and Decision-Making Across 21,000 Autonomous Schools? Learning from the Journey in England, in Brown, C (ed) *Leading the Use of Research and Evidence in Schools*. London: Institute of Education Press.

Griffith, A and Burns, M (2014) *Outstanding Teaching: Teaching Backwards*. Carmarthen: Crown House.

Hargreaves, A (1994) *Changing Teachers, Changing Times: Teachers Work and Culture in the Postmodern Age*. London and New York: Continuum.

Hargreaves, A (1996) *Teaching as a Research-Based Profession: Possibilities and Prospect: The Teacher Training Agency Lecture 1996*. London: TTA.

Hargreaves, A and Fullan, M (2012) *Professional Capital: Transforming Teaching in Every School*. New York: Teachers College Press.

Harris, A (2014) *Distributed Leadership Matters: Perspectives, Practicalities, and Potential*. London, New Delhi, Singapore: Corwin/Sage.

Harris, A and Muijs, D (2005) *Improving Schools Through Teacher Leadership*. Maidenhead, Two Penn Plazs, New York: Open University Press.

James, C and Oplatka, I (2015) An Exploration of the Notion of the 'Good Enough School'. *Management in Education*, 29(2): 77–82.

Jones, V and Brazdau, O (2015) Conscious Leadership, A Reciprocal Connected Practice. A Qualitative Study on Postsecondary Education. *Procedia – Social and Behavioral Sciences*, 203: 251–6.

Lear, J (2015) *Guerilla Teaching: Revolutionary Tactics for Teachers on the Ground, in Real Classrooms, Working with Real Children, Trying to Make a Real Difference.* Carmarthen: Independent Thinking Press.

McIntyre, J and Hobson, A (2015) Supporting Beginner Teacher Identity Development: External Mentors and the Third Space. *Research Papers in Education*, 31(2): 133–58.

Mockler, N and Groundwater-Smith, S (2015) Seeking Unwelcome Truths: Beyond Celebration in Inquiry-Based Teacher Professional Learning. *Teachers and teaching: Theory and Practice,* 21(5), 603–14.

Moss, J (2008) Leading Professional Learning in an Australian Secondary School Through School–University Partnerships. *Asia-Pacific Journal of Teacher Education*, 36(4): 345–57.

Nelson, J and O'Beirne, C (2014) *Using Evidence in the Classroom: What Works and Why?* Slough NFER.

NFER (2015) Self-Review Tool for Research Engagement in Schools. [online] Available at: www.nfer. ac.uk/schools/research-in-schools/self-review-tool-for-research-engagement-in-schools/ (accessed 27 January 2017).

Oancea, A and Pring, R (2009) The Importance of Being Thorough, in Bridges, D, Smeyers, P. and Smith, R. (eds) *Evidence-Based Education Policy: What Evidence? What Basis? Whose Policy?* Chichester: Wiley-Blackwell.

Orland-Barak, L (2009) Unpacking Variety in Practitioner Inquiry on Teaching and Teacher Education. *Educational Action Research*, 17(1): 111–19.

Peterson, L (1998) *Anyone Can Be Cool … But Awesome Takes Practice.* Motor City Books.

Platten, R (n d) The Fight Song. [online] Available at: www.youtube.com/watch?v=xo1VInw-SKc (accessed 24 January 2017).

Postholm, M B (2009) Research and Development Work: Developing Teachers as Researchers or Just Teachers? *Educational Action Research*, 17(4): 551–65.

Poultney, V (2015) *'Whoa This Is Massive, This Is Huge': Leading the Inquiry-Focused Primary School.* Conference presentation, University of Derby Teaching and Learning Conference, Buxton.

Poultney, V (2016) The Self-Improving Primary School: Understanding and Approaching Teacher Inquiry: A Pilot Study. *TEAN Journal*, 8(1): 83–93. http://194.81.189.19/ojs/index.php/TEAN/article/viewFile/290/415.

Rooke J (2012) *Transforming Writing: Interim Evaluation Report.* London: National Literacy Trust, Esmee Fairbairn Foundation.

Ryan, W and Gilbert, I (eds) (2011) *Inspirational Teachers Inspirational Learners: A Book of Hope for Creativity and the Curriculum in the Twenty First Century.* Carmarthen: Crown House Publishing.

Salles, D (2016) *The Slightly Awesome Teacher: Ed-Research Meets Common Sense.* Woodbridge: John Catt Educational.

Sebba, J, Kent, P and Treganza, J (2012) *Powerful Professional Learning: A School Leader's Guide to Joint Professional Development.* National College for School Leadership. [online] Available at: www.gov.uk/government/uploads/system/uploads/attachment_data/file/329717/powerful-professional-learning-a-school-leaders-guide-to-joint-practice-development.pdf (accessed 18 January 2017).

Sharp, C, Eames, A, Sanders, D and Tomlinson, K (2006) Leading a Research Engaged School. *National College for School Leadership (NCSL).* [online] Available at: www.silkalliance.org.uk/docs/r&d/Leading_a_research_engaged_school.pdf (accessed 7 March 2017).

Sheard, M K and Sharples, J (2016) School Leaders' Engagement with the Concept of Evidence-Based Practice as a Management Tool for School Improvement. *Educational Management Administration and Leadership*, 44(4): 668–87.

Skattebol, J and Arthur, L M (2014) Collaborative Practitioner Research: Opening a Third Space for Local Knowledge Production. *Asia-Pacific Journal of Teacher Education*, 34(3): 351–65.

Southworth, G (2000) How Primary Schools Learn. *Research Papers in Education*, 15(3): 275–91.

Stenhouse, L (1975) *An Introduction to Curriculum Research and Development*. London: Heinemann.

Stoll, L (2009) Capacity Building for School Improvement or Creating Capacity for Learning? A Changing Landscape. *Journal of Educational Change*, 10(2–3): 115–27.

Stoll, L (2015) Three Greats for a Self-Improving School System – Pedagogy, Professional Development and Leadership: Teaching Schools R & D Network National Themes Project 2012–14. National College for Teaching and Leadership. [online] Available at: www.gov.uk/government/uploads/system/uploads/attachment_data/file/406278/Three_greats_for_a_self_improving_system_pedagogy_professional_development_and_leadership_full_report.pdf (accessed 23 January 2017).

Swift, T (2014) Shake It Off. [online] Available at: www.youtube.com/watch?v=nfWlot6h_JM (accessed 12 July 2016).

INDEX